The Path to Odin's Lake

By Jason Heppenstall

Copyright © Jason Heppenstall 2015

Original woodcut cover art by Pernille Christensen

Edited by Palden Jenkins

2nd edition published May 2015

The previous page depicts the Norse Valknut, a symbol associated with the god Odin and his followers.

ISBN-13: 978-1511711401

ISBN-10: 151171140X

Ǫnd þau né átto, óð þau né hǫfðo,
lá né læti né lito góða.
Ǫnd gaf Óðinn, óð gaf Hœnir,
lá gaf Lóðurr ok lito góða.

Spirit they possessed not, sense they had not,
blood nor motive powers, nor goodly colour.
Spirit gave Odin, sense gave Hœnir,
blood gave Lodur, and goodly colour.

From the epic poem Völuspá, translated by Benjamin
Thorpe, in which Odin speaks with the völva shaman and
foresees Ragnarök - the destruction of the world before it
is reborn anew.

Acknowledgements

With many thanks to those whom I met on my journey and helped me in one way or another even if they didn't intend to. Special appreciation goes to my family for putting up with me, to Pernille Christensen for her artwork and to Palden Jenkins for editing the manuscript, pointing out my errors in Swedish and generally making it more readable.

In this book I have quoted extensively from Bill Plotkin's *Soulcraft*, published by New World Library, as well as Marcus Aurelius's *Meditations*, translated by Martin Hammond and published by Penguin Classics.

Everything I recount in this story actually happened, although some names and details of people and organisations have been changed for reasons of privacy.

Prologue

The email from my mother-in-law came at exactly the right time. I had spent the summer struggling to finish writing a book. It was to be about peak oil, the decline of industrial civilisation, climate change and other light-hearted topics. I hoped that by writing such a book I might somehow be able to make a few people take note of these things and change their lives accordingly. But the book was going nowhere fast. I had contacted a few publishers to see if they might be interested. Most said they were not interested although one said they might consider it if I proposed a solution or two at the end.

But that was just the bind. My book didn't offer any solutions. No cavalry was coming to rescue us at the last minute if only we all did this or that. I had come to this unwelcome conclusion after years of consideration. During that time I had collected enough books on the downward spiral of industrial civilisation to make the shelves groan under their weight. I had eagerly read them and participated in online discussions with like-minded people, even writing my own blog on the topic of the end of the age of abundance. I had talked the talk and backed it up by walking the walk, quitting my well-paid office job, getting out of debt and downsizing my life to one that didn't require massive throughputs of energy.

Friends considered my actions and used words like 'eccentric'. Others were less polite. Some said I was a luddite, a doomer and I wanted everyone to live in caves and wear scratchy woollen jumpers. But most of all, people simply said I was 'mistaken'. They said that technology would fix most of the problems we had created, and that even if it couldn't we would one day simply travel to a virgin planet and once again set about the task of converting its resources into consumer products.

Five years previously I had read a book, which had led to

another book, which had in turn led to a kind of epiphany. The realisation was that our civilisation was heading for a messy descent of crisis piled on top of crisis that would come to dominate the rest of our lives. Of course, most people recognised this on some subconscious level, but suddenly the timescale of its unravelling seemed to have speeded up markedly. This wasn't something that could be easily shunted onto our grandchildren – it was going to hit us right now. What's more, our way of living was threatening to alter and degrade much of the biosphere in the process. The more I learned, the more worrying it all became. Peak oil, climate change, mass extinctions, ocean acidification, mega-droughts, religious fundamentalism, militarisation and accumulating toxic pollution – each of these things was worrisome enough on its own, but the realisation that all of these things were interrelated and converging at speed was the most unsettling aspect.

People said I shouldn't worry. They employed thought-stoppers to put an end to such conversations. "They'll think of something", they said. "People have been saying that the world would end for centuries", or "It's all a conspiracy of the press and the global elite". "It won't happen in our lifetimes." It was perhaps understandable that people would want to look away and pretend that none of it mattered, but this was hardly an effective strategy for survival. Indeed, some people said "I'll be dead before any of that happens, so why worry?".

But I didn't think the world would end. That was not my conclusion. I had, however, drawn together enough strands to make a best guess at the situation, and my assessment told me that things were going to get tough, very tough. And soon. I was worried. Not so much for my own sake but for that of my children. For everyone's children. And for the delicate web of life on Earth that we seem so intent on unravelling.

This was tough going, mentally. I scoured news websites daily, looking for cracks in the edifice of the global industrial system. The more I looked the more rickety the whole structure seemed. It seemed as if we were living in a wriggling morass of lies, deceit, propaganda, fear and cargo cults. This depressed me, making me want to numb my feelings. But another part of me refused to be subdued. I felt that we had to somehow get out of 'the system'.

So we moved to live amidst the wild beauty of Cornwall, buying a small patch of woodland to turn into a living example of an alternative to the nature exploitation I saw all around. It was to be a place humming with life and hope, a tonic for mental and physical health, and an insurance policy against the kind of socioeconomic collapse that seemed inevitable. I had decided that the only rational way to deal with the dire situation facing the world was to, in the words of Gandhi, *be the change*. It seemed like a futile gesture in all probability, and the last thing I wanted to be thought of was 'worthy'. But it was either that or continue to fritter the years away supporting a system that made things worse rather than better.

But opting out of a large part of the system also had its drawbacks. Foreign travel, a lifelong interest for me, had become unaffordable. I had few regrets about this because since stepping outside of the system my life had become immeasurably richer. Nevertheless, I found myself harbouring a yearning to just simply get away from it all. For several years I had experienced a growing longing to step outside of the human-centred world and wander off into the wilderness. I don't mean that I wanted to disappear permanently, like the ill-fated Christopher McCandless whose story was told in the film *Into the Wild*. No, I simply wanted to escape for a while to readjust my perspective and clean my mental lenses.

A scene from a dream kept repeating itself to me. In it I was standing on a mountain ridge looking down on a sprawling town set in a rugged landscape. I felt sure that the place I was looking at was somewhere in Scotland, or maybe Norway. From this high vantage point I could observe the people scurrying around in their busy lives, hear the gossip, the chatter about last night's television, and feel their insecurities about their mortgages, their pensions, their place in the world. What's more, I could see a kind of foggy miasma wafting up from the town into the sky above. The toxic smog didn't seem visible to the people below, but it was all too clear to me standing on that ridge. I felt alarmed at the way the people in the town appeared trapped, unable to step back for a moment and look at the situation in which they lived. Up on my lofty eyrie it seemed that my observations did not go unnoticed, and it felt as if there was a conversation to be had with something or someone, but that this conversation was always cut short before it could even begin.

Admittedly, it wasn't much of a dream, but I remembered the keen feelings of escape it invoked within me. I wanted to live out my vision and something inside me told me that I would learn something of value if I did so. Henry David Thoreau once expressed such a sentiment when he wrote: "*I went to the woods because I wished to live deliberately, to front only the essential facts of life, and see if I could not learn what it had to teach, and not, when I came to die, discover that I had not lived*".

That's pretty much how I felt too. But such an escape seemed unlikely, to say the least. I had commitments. There were the kids, who needed me around in the summer holiday, some freelance translation jobs that screamed out for completion, various projects at the woodland, urgent repairs to our old house that needed doing before winter... the damned book to finish. It felt as if I would never get a chance to experience that dream.

The realisation that I wouldn't get this chance to finish the conversation saddened me. Instead of writing my book I found myself gazing out of the window across the bay to St Michael's Mount sitting in its silvery sea. I thought about its Cornish, pre-Christian, name *Karrek Loos yn Koos*, meaning *the rock in the woods,* and how, during the turbulent storms of the previous winter the sea bed had been scoured clean to reveal the stumps of trees thousands of years old. The island had been a trading post, a place where tin was sold to Mycenaeans during the bronze age, and as such had played its part in the rise of classical Greek civilisation and therefore our own civilisation too. Legend has it that Jesus set foot there, and local geomancers said that the island was a major node for unseen lines of energy coursing around the planet. The view of the mount, with the rolling waves from the bay crashing against its rocky shore, made me reflective. It made me think about our own precarious existence, about how fleeting and precious it is when set within the long count of time.

And then the email from my mother-in-law in Copenhagen popped up in my inbox. Our children would be going to stay with her for two weeks at the end of summer. That much I knew already, but she went on to say that the airline was refusing to allow them to travel unaccompanied, that they would need an adult to fly with them. Would I, she asked, travel with them? She would, of course, pay for all my travel.

"I think it would be a good idea", said my wife, who was fully booked with work commitments and could not make the journey herself. "You could go around the businesses in Copenhagen and try to drum up some translation work."

"I could indeed…", I replied, glancing at the map of Scandinavia on the wall above my desk with its vast open spaces, its crenelated coastlines and its rugged mountain interior.

Or I could do something else entirely, I thought…

Chapter 1. Ejected

"It is not the path which is the difficulty. It is the difficulty which is the path."

– Søren Kierkegaard

And so, one Sunday morning in late summer, just as a fire seemed to be taking a hold of the world, I looked down from the food court and saw sea creatures. They swam, either individually or in shoals. Some pulsated while others slithered as they moved between the black-slimed outcrops of concrete. Strands of seaweed waved gently in the ocean current and clusters of shellfish – mussels, limpets and clams – crowded the fissures and coated the rigid headless human bodies that littered the seabed like broken plastic starfish.

Through these watery ruins there wandered ghosts. Their shadowy figures drifted aimlessly over the sandy sea floor, faces fixed in masks of calm equanimity as they moved alone or in pairs. Some of them were pushing children in buggies while others gazed at the small barnacle-encrusted rectangles they were holding at belly-height.

Around me were the sounds of the sea – the cry of gulls on the wind and the slooping roll of the waves as they folded upon the shore. But mingled with these sounds of nature were other sounds; the tinkling of porcelain cups and saucers, and the faint echo of dreamy music to which the seaweed seemed to be moving its frond-like arms as if at some concert from another world or another time. I raised my camera and focused it on the scene below, although I knew the lens would not capture what I was seeing.

"What are you doing?" said a male voice. I shifted my gaze from the scene around me and brought the man into focus. A security guard. He stood at my side and looked at me accusingly.

"I'm just taking some photographs", I said, rather obviously. Although it had crossed my mind that the simple act of capturing reflections of light on a microchip in this place might be a tiny bit subversive, it had not stopped me from wandering around and doing so for the last half hour.

"You'll have to leave", he said. "You're not permitted." I looked at him. Stocky. He was wearing a sand-coloured uniform with short sleeves that clung tightly to his inky biceps. His face was lined, but not with wisdom or age. A razor sharp line of beard cut down either side of his face and in one ear he wore a communications device which sprouted a thin microphonic arm that reached towards his mouth like a spidery limb.

"Come with me", he said.

I walked at his side, fiddling to put the lens cap back on my camera. "I'm sorry, I was just daydreaming", I said. "I was about to leave."

"Good", said the guard. "One of the store managers called about you."

It was true. I had been wandering around this Copenhagen shopping mall – said to be the grandest in all of Scandinavia – taking pictures of the effigies. They were arranged behind the plate-glass windows, some with heads but many without, some with black glittery plastic skin, yet others with hard white faces lacking eyes, noses or mouths. In one store half a dozen headless children wore items from the autumn fashion collection as they hung from the ceiling on wires. Snap. There was astroturf in the window of the Body Shop on which a synthetic rabbit held up a sign saying *Cruelty Free*. Snap. Framed in another a plastic cow grazed on plastic grass beside a sign that said *Get back to Nature!* Snap. No wonder this place was inducing hallucinatory dreams in me.

"This way", said my ejector.

As far as I could see the only living organisms in here were the shoppers themselves. Even potted tropical plants were absent.

I stepped onto the metal escalator which conveyed consumers from the food court on the top level down past the fashion level and onto the ground floor. Down here, in the first circle of the mall, it was mostly shops selling gadgets and computer games. Teenage boys and men clutched shiny polythene bags as they wandered about, their faces rapt and expressionless. *Have you bought your Back to School iPad?* asked a giant blue cartoon shark. In another window a muscular cardboard marine wearing a death skull mask pointed an automatic weapon at me and said *Coming Soon.*

"Why are you carrying that?", asked the guard.

"It's a staff", I replied. "To help me walk."

He uttered a disapproving snort. Maybe he was not comfortable with me holding a six-foot piece of wood – perhaps he had watched too many kung fu movies. I told him how I had cut it that morning, that it was a rowan ash sapling and that it would grow back in time.

As we approached the big revolving doors he seemed to ease up a little. In a few moments I would be gone from his realm, vanished from sight and transformed into an SEP (someone else's problem). "Where are you walking to?"

"Sweden", I replied. We had reached the large revolving doors – the type that you are not supposed to touch as they move around as it will make them stop, although many people do. *"God tur"*, he said in Danish, meaning 'have a good journey', ejecting me from the sterile cathedral of consumption into the dirty but real dimension of fresh air, trees and unstructured time where plastic cows don't eat plastic grass and flesh and blood rabbits somehow live

12

with the cruelty of the world.

This was going to be an interesting journey, of that I felt sure.

Chapter 2. Copenhagenised

"It is warm work; and this day may be the last to any of us at a moment. But mark you! I would not be elsewhere for thousands."

– Admiral Horatio Nelson at the Battle of Copenhagen

Earlier that same morning I had kissed my two daughters goodbye as they lay sleeping and quietly left the house. The suburban streets had been silent and empty as I walked to the metro station. It was only a twenty minute walk but my rucksack already seemed too heavy. Had I packed too much? In it was a small tent, some clothes, food to last a few days and two reading books. There were some cooking and eating utensils, maps and a small blow-up mattress. A sleeping bag dangled free from the back of my pack and I had another small bag strapped to my front with a camera, waterproof clothing, a Swiss army knife and a hand-forged Swedish Gränsfors axe. The axe was there for firewood, and maybe security.

By the time I reached the station a sea mist had rolled in, muffling my footsteps and cloaking the flat landscape in an eerie fog. Around a dozen other people were waiting for the fully-automatic driverless train to turn up. All were plugged into and absorbed by their smartphones – all except one youth who was dressed anarchically as a punk in black leathers and wore a spiky dog collar around his throat. He was shouting obscenities at the ether as he took swigs from a bottle of vodka. Everyone ignored him. I thought it unusual to spot a punk in Denmark and I didn't recall seeing one before. Perhaps it was simply a new fashion.

The train arrived and people looked up from their smart-phones momentarily. We got on it. The punk sat down nearby, slumped on a folding seat and growling incoherently. People continued to ignore him and an invisible bubble was created around his presence. We glided smoothly on high rails past the modern symphony hall as it rose up out of the mist and the punk swayed to the rhythm of the train. The bottle fell from his limp hand and rolled around on the floor. Presently a young woman went over to him, put an arm around him with sisterly tenderness and whispered something in his ear. This seemed to calm him and he sat there looking at the space between his feet for the rest of the journey as if enchanted. The young woman went back to her seat and I was left wondering what kind of magic she possessed.

We pulled into the underground station at Kongens Nytorv and I ascended the steps to the daylight. This elegant square held so many memories for me and I stood for a few minutes simply allowing the feelings they evoked to run their course. There was Hviids Vinstue, where I had spent so many evenings drinking porter ale with my newspaper buddies, and there was the office we had worked in – the same office where some cartoons of Mohammed had been published and poured petrol on a flaming world. And there was the old opera house where I had bluffed reviews of things I knew nothing about.

On the other side lay the canal district of Nyhavn where I used to eat raw herrings and drink schnaps made from wild berries; the cafe where we would moan about our office colleagues; the imposing Hotel D'Angleterre where I had met the Dalai Lama and felt a charge of energy run up my arm when we shook hands. There were good memories and bad ones, bittersweet ones and sweet bitter ones. I gave myself a minute more and then set off down Strøget, the pedestrian street, as the tolling bells of the Church of the Holy Spirit rang out over the city, calling the pious to Sunday prayer.

A quarter of an hour later I was standing in the city hall square before the imposing Rådhus, resplendent in its Italianate grandeur. The sky was blue and the air crisply chill as small groups of tourists walked past and a woman struggled to set up her mobile hotdog stall. Traffic on the adjacent Hans Christian Andersens Boulevard was light, and the joyfully ebullient facade of Tivoli Gardens reflected the morning sun back at me. It had been some eighteen years since I had first set foot in this square, and ten of those had been spent living in this city. On my first visit I remembered being hustled into the Rådhus by my excited future father-in-law who said "Look, you must come and see, you are inside!". He was, it turned out, referring to the statue of Jason, of Argonaut fame, created by the sculptor Bertel Thorvaldsen in Denmark's long-gone golden age.

But today I could have done with a dose of heroism in my heart. Uncertainty and anxiety played on my nerves and I felt was that I wasn't entirely sure what I was doing and why I was about to do it. All journeys, I reasoned, must have a starting point and an end point. I wasn't sure where the end point of my journey would be, but at least I could pick the start point. If, as I had planned, I would proceed from a point of civilisation to a point of uncivilisation, then this place was as good as any to start out from. I shouldered my pack, tightened the straps across my chest and clicked the plastic waist buckle into place. And then I set off.

I walked down the six lane boulevard. Cyclists wobbled lazily past me, some of them looking like they were on their way home from the night before. I had considered walking straight across the Langebro bridge which separates the main part of the city from the island of Amager, but now I chose to veer off to the south, keeping the narrow channel of seawater on my left. I would, I decided, take the indirect route and pass through the city's red light district and eventually out into an area of wild scrubland on the far side of Islands Brygge (Iceland Quay).

As the cyclists streamed past me I felt a pang. In all the time I had lived here I calculated that I had biked the city's famed cycle lanes to an equivalent distance of pedalling all the way to Australia. In this city a bike was all you needed to get you from door to door for free, whether that door is your front door, an office door or a pub door. Perhaps I should be on two wheels now, I considered. It would certainly be easier than walking.

I carried on down the steps beside the channel and continued to the central train station, emerging from the other side of its capacious hall into the seedier side of town. Drunks hung around on the steps and I walked up Istegade with its shop windows crammed full of dildos and bondage gear. A few dispirited looking Nigerian prostitutes hung around and eyed me languidly. They didn't approach me, or hiss "Good time, mistah?" as they had sometimes done during my past life when I was on my way to the office with a laptop bag slung over my shoulder. I went by the 'men's home' where there was always a posse of ragged-looking characters outside drinking Carlsberg Special Brew.

On a whim I turned down a side street, seeking out a place well known to me. There, on a corner, was a small Chinese restaurant, closed at this hour. Some vermillion characters stood above the glass door and my reflection looked back at me from within. I was transported back in time to an evening here five years before.

***

It had been early evening and I sat alone, pushing a steamed bun around my bowl with a chopstick. You could usually find me here early on a Tuesday evening killing time between leaving the office and doing my Tai Chi class. It was a kind of weekly treat that I looked forward to. Beside me on the table was a copy of John Michael

17

Greer's book *The Long Descent: A User's Guide to the End of the Industrial Age*, which I had just finished reading. Outside, in the first warm spring evening of the year, gangs of hooded men stood on street corners as police patrol cars occasionally crawled past.

I was having difficulty enjoying myself this evening. Perhaps I was feeling a bit melancholy and sensitised after reading *The Long Descent*, which examines our human predicament through an historical and ecological paradigm. This was no shrill denunciation of modernity, being instead a carefully stated riposte to the fantasies of everlasting prosperity and technological progress that seemed to fuel the modern imagination. I'm not sure what the opposite of a lullaby is, but *The Long Descent* would seem to be it.

Nobody could seriously read Greer's concise prose and come to a happy conclusion without resorting to extreme mental contortions. How does one live with the knowledge that in the next century or so the ecological basis of our civilisation will dissolve with mathematical certainty and the vast majority of us will be dragged down with it? How is it possible to hold such knowledge in mind and still manage to live a normal life in a culture which tells us that the most important news is the release of the latest consumer electronics gadget? There's no point taking your thoughts and feelings to a psychiatrist as they'll either put you on mind-altering pills or suggest therapy to help you get over it.

No, there is no way to internalise the concepts of overshoot and die-off and still maintain a state of mental happiness – a state of depression seems to be the only rational option for the non-sociopathic. I was put in mind of a recent study which concluded that mildly depressed people were much more likely to be aware of the scale of our ecological problems than the non-depressed. My immediate thought at the time was that it could well be the other way around. In any case there was little comfort to be found in the study's findings.

Finishing my dim sum I got up and paid. It was still too early for my class so I decided to walk instead of bike across the city. I pushed my bike past the battered-looking prostitutes, the crack dealers and the derelict Greenlanders and yet despite the fresh spring air I felt an all too familiar sinking feeling. Because there, juxtaposed against the human wrecks, sat all the shiny, happy well-adjusted young urbanites, talking into their smartphones, drinking tall glasses of lager and wine and looking for all the world like there was no problem with anything anywhere. Their presence was an enigma to me, their levity of being at odds with my depressed state. Perhaps it was just me, I considered. Perhaps I was the maladjusted one who didn't know how to enjoy himself.

That evening I decided to cut across town through a park I had never explored before. I felt in need of some greenery – perhaps that would cheer me up a bit I thought. The park, Frederiksberg Have, was erupting with snowdrops and other spring flowers when I arrived. Why had I never been here before? It was beautiful. I immediately felt something righting itself within me as I walked through stands of spreading beech trees and past the ornamental lakes.

The city, with its frenetic traffic and its 7-Elevens, disappeared from view and, beyond the trees, the only buildings to be seen were the elegant apartment blocks built in the nineteenth century. I gazed at them beyond the trees as the light from the setting sun illuminated their facades and turned them the colour of honey. The grace displayed in their design came from a time now past. Nothing of any such beauty has been built for a hundred years in this city, although nobody could adequately explain why.

Yet the buildings, and indeed the beautifully landscaped park, were all the result of a kind of apocalypse that had struck the city two centuries earlier. It had been the time of the Napoleonic Wars and Denmark, proclaiming neutrality, was about to receive a nasty shock. I'm not sure if any

British admiral used the phrase "You're either with us or against us", but it was decided in London that the best course of action to take against the untrustworthy Danes was to sail a fleet of British gunboats into Copenhagen harbour and reduce the city to a pile of smouldering rubble. When the gunships arrived the bombardment commenced without warning and continuing for several nights.

This act of total war was the first example of a pre-emptive strike aimed at a civilian population using ballistic weapons. The British gunboats used Congreve rockets, designed to spread fire and, by the end of it, around two thousand citizens lay dead and the city was in ruins. As a final act the British navy confiscated the Danish navy's entire fleet of ships and set fire to those they couldn't navigate back to England. This last tactic was such a success and the razing of Copenhagen so complete that a new verb was coined to properly express it – to *Copenhagenise*.

But from this cataclysm, like a phoenix from the ashes, something amazing occurred. The city was rebuilt from the ground up, with wide boulevards and spacious parks such as the one in which I was now walking. The arts flourished, with painters and sculptors becoming household names, and writers, such as Hans Christian Andersen and Søren Kierkegaard, gave the world respectively heartbreaking morality tales and existential philosophy. A new Golden Age was ushered in.

Returning to the present, could our pending catastrophe give rise to something similar? It didn't look likely. Europe in the nineteenth century could thank rampant industrialism, cheap energy and ever-concentrating power to bring in the resources to build on such a vast scale. Huge sums of money had been lavished on Italian and French artisans to design the wonderful architecture and no scheme was considered too grand. It was as if nineteenth century Europe, with its colonial possessions, was pushing against an open door. Could such a phenomenon occur today? No, the twin realities of resource depletion and the dimming of energy supplies mean that the shops have sold out of Golden Ages for the time being, possibly forever.

I walked on through the park, savouring the warm air and the calm atmosphere. Above, in some very tall trees, hundreds of jackdaws were having a very loud meeting. I stood still and watched them, observing their behaviour. They would take it in turns to fly off in small groups, wheel around the flock as a whole and then return to the branches. All the while they collectively emitted a cacophony, but every now and again a silence would come over them for some seconds, and then the noisy din would start up again. What were they doing? I watched in wonder for about five minutes, noticing after a while that the park had emptied of joggers.

I walked away, happy to have been reminded that there are other worlds outside the human one we are often so caught up in. As I walked away towards the park exit I saw two young girls in summer dresses kneeling down on the grass picking the snowdrops near a sign that said 'Keep off the Grass'. There was nobody else around – just me, the flower-collecting girls and several hundred jackdaws. I decided not to bother with Tai Chi after all. Instead I wanted to go home and tuck up my own two daughters in bed, read them a bedtime story. As I rode home through the darkening city streets I thought to myself how lucky I was to be alive, to smell the first scent of spring on the breeze, to allow myself to be mesmerised by the murmurations of jackdaws as the sun sank low in the west and the city buildings cast their long shadows.

***

These were the memories I had as I stood outside that small Chinese restaurant in the seedy side of town on that clear Sunday morning at the end of summer.

Chapter 3. Pitch invader

"The more clearly we can focus our attention on the wonders and realities of the universe about us, the less taste we shall have for destruction."

– Rachel Carson

Turning my back on the Chinese restaurant I walked further up Istegade, I took a left and swung past the meat-packing district to which the office my old newspaper had been relocated after the Mohammed cartoon furore. It had only been later that we discovered the former office had been targeted by truck bombers. I was lucky to be alive. We had relocated to an old slaughterhouse and it was this part of town that planners were keen to turn into a post-industrial playground for hipsters and moneyed young service sector workers.

I didn't have any desire to stop and hang around in Vesterbro. Its junkies and its trafficked girls made me feel raw and nervy, and anyway I didn't want to bump into anyone I knew and have to explain myself. Carrying on, I walked to the waterfront shopping development at Fisketorv and crossed over the channel on a narrow bridge built for pedestrians and cyclists. On the other side I sat down and rested by the water.

It's difficult to walk through the centre of Copenhagen and attempt to describe it without sounding like a travel guide. Many things, it seems, are for show and the bits that are not for show are rarely mentioned. Indeed, I had written pieces for in-flight airline magazines with remits such as 'List ten reasons why Copenhagen is wonderful'. Everyone understood that this was an industry, an industry of creative illusions.

But to me Copenhagen was more than its dull 'wonderful-ness'. It was a real place, and not just a city stuffed with PR flacks whose job it was to boost tourism and inward investment. It was here in this city that my two daughters had been born, that I worked some of the worst jobs in my life, and also the best. I loved its cycling culture, its clean air and water, its beaches and its restaurants. But some-thing didn't quite chime and, for me, it always felt like a place to be passing through, a waiting zone where life is a dream, with real life happening somewhere else.

As the fantasy vision of the city fades only then can one see its truer aspects. The poverty of its inner ghettos comes into focus, along with the tower blocks, its spiritless outer suburbs and the smouldering gang warfare with its occa-sional bloody killings. And then there were the galloping egos of the new wave of architects with their ludicrous designs. The glass and steel buildings they flung up were stuffed with PR firms and advertising agencies, corporate media and firms making computer games or IT solutions. These buildings were filled with people who ate in high-end Michelin starred restaurants and vied with one another over matters of status. Once, I met a group of internet ar-chitects who chartered a plane and flew their whole office to a private island in Thailand for the weekend. No excess was considered too great for them and yet they could never fully explain exactly what it was they produced or why it had such value.

During my time writing about the city's food scene I had enjoyed dining in fine restaurants but the sycophancy soon got me down. One meal, at an Italian place, served us a twelve-course meal with wine pairings that would have cost the astronomical sum of five thousand kroner (about £600 at the time) had we paid for it. It seemed unworthy of mention that in the streets outside wandered destitute Greenlanders, wasted on cheap beer and vodka, and that they were rarely mentioned in this most egalitarian of nations. More ghosts.

I tried to get an invite to Noma, voted the world's best restaurant several years in a row, but the owner said he had no need for publicity. A paying friend went instead one day and told me he had been served a single live prawn in a glass of melted iceberg water, and a plant with a pot of soil, which one was expected to eat. I was all in favour of a resurgence in Nordic fare but I wasn't sure how charging the well-heeled large sums of money to drink a living prawn furthered its cause.

For me, Copenhagen had become a shadow city. It was a place for good-timers, party central for the loaded generation, and a hall of mirrors. The illusions confused me - all the talk of being 'green' in this nation with the fourth largest ecological footprint in the world per person. I had an uneasy feeling about the place - it felt as if something bad was coming - and so we had left Copenhagen. Simply put, the 'happiest people on Earth' would just have to get along without us. We bought a large trailer to put all our stuff in and drove and drove until we could not drive any further without falling into the Atlantic Ocean. We pulled to a stop at the far end of Cornwall, a place that had been calling to me since childhood.

And now I was back again for a valedictory tour. I gazed out over the blue water at the tapering brick towers of this generally low-rise city that had been founded by a bishop on a piece of mosquito-infested swampland, and I said a last *farvel*. Hauling my pack up onto my back again I trudged onwards through new apartment developments towards the outer crust of the city. Soon I found myself in the hinterland of Amager Fælled, a large scrubby area of woods and fields criss-crossed with cycle lanes and footpaths. Sunday morning joggers overtook me as I traversed the tarmac surface that wove between dense ranks of thorny bushes and small trees. Shiny-looking families were out walking with their well-groomed dogs and their well-scrubbed young children. It was like a commercial for life insurance.

I looked out of place in this environment. I confess that I didn't cut a dapper figure, clad as I was in dirty cut-off jeans and old walking shoes, and with an unkempt beard, sunglasses and a filthy old baseball cap I had purchased from a market in Spain for one euro. To top it off I had an open gash on my knee from falling off a granite wall in Cornwall a few days before, and this was surrounded by purple bruises and pinkish skin. When I thought about it I could probably have passed for one of the central station heroin addicts. I must have appeared as an outcast in this tame wilderness and it was probably no wonder that some of the parents were giving me suspicious glances and placing a protective hand on their children's shoulders as I passed.

After walking for another twenty minutes or so I dodged into a clearing between some bushes and put down my pack. What I needed, I thought, was a staff. A staff would not just help me to walk, it would indicate to others that I was a walker with a purpose, rather than a drifter. I scanned the area and found a rowan ash sapling with a nice straight trunk. From my pack I took out the sharp axe and chopped the tree down a few inches from the ground. I apologised to the stump for this violation, but I knew it would grow back the next spring. I then proceeded to sned the side branches with the axe, which was more of a hatchet really, and before long I had a strong walking staff about six feet in length.

I emerged from the clearing and carried on heading in an easterly direction. I knew that I would be walking for only an hour or so before I hit the outskirts of the new development of Ørestad and, in fact, I could already see the Field's shopping mall in the distance, as well as the Daliesque double towers of the Bella Sky hotel. Before long the trees and bushes gave way to cement trucks and concrete bollards, and I was walking the immaculate new streets of Ørestad and ascending the steps to Field's shopping mall.

Half an hour later I was back on those same steps with the security guard stood by the revolving door, his arms folded across his chest. I walked away and headed out across an area of wasteland where they were planning to build the new national football stadium. Out front was a large sign detailing the development, but despite there being several vans and trucks visible there didn't seem to be anyone around today. I squeezed through a ripped-open section of fence and wandered onto the construction site. Judging by the dimensions of the place I figured where the likely centre of the future pitch would be and wandered over to it.

Sitting down, I set about making a small fire from twigs on which to set my little saucepan and metal stove ring. Yes, it was time for tea. As the flames crackled and the water started to heat I lay back and looked around. It being late summer the wild plants and flowers had grown exuberantly and were tall enough to shield me from anyone looking in. What's more, they blotted out the various shopping centres, hotels and conference halls that had sprung up over recent years in the area.

I picked a handful of sea buckthorn berries from a bush and popped them into my mouth. The juice was sweet and tangy and I picked some more. As I ate them I looked around at the other plants. It was like being in a jungle on some alien planet. The sheer brightness and refulgence was dazzling, with multitudes of blues, purples, yellows and reds vying for the attention of the bees which flew from flower to flower, their legs hung heavy with sticky yellow pollen. I got down on my elbows and looked more closely at one who was resting on a drooping purple flower. Entering his world it seemed like a miniature paradise for him, and he looked drunk on nectar as he staggered around on the flower head, his abdomen pulsating as if he were out of breath from the exertion of collecting the pollen. What tales, I wondered, could he tell me if we would just speak the same language? Perhaps he could tell us how we could save his species, and maybe ourselves too.

The water in the pan had boiled and I dropped in a teabag and made myself a brew. Sipping the hot drink I took out the notebook I had brought with me and sketched the flower and the bee. But I'm not much of an artist and the drawing came out crudely. Instead I wrote a few words about what had happened so far on my journey, even though I was only several hours into it. I had decided that this trip would be as low-tech as possible. Like many people, I had become far more used to typing words on a keyboard than writing them on a page, and my hand felt slightly clumsy as I wrote the words with a ballpoint pen. I wrote about the punk on the train, cutting the staff, meeting the security guard. When I was satisfied that I'd made a reasonable account I closed the diary and put it away again.

I drank my tea and marvelled at all this richness that was scheduled for demolition. The only slight consolation of its impending destruction would be a future me watching some international football match on television and knowing that I had drunk tea and communed with the bees somewhere within the circumference of the centre circle. With this thought in my head I packed up my things, said goodbye to the bees and set off south again. Before long I was at the gates of the Amager Fælled nature reserve, a pan flat area of fields, birch woods and reedy drainage ditches that had been reclaimed from the sea after the last world war. It would be a long plod going south over the next few hours as the sun beat down on me.

The path was straight and narrow. Cyclists zoomed past me on carbon-fibre bikes as I walked. These weren't the meandering, lazy city cyclists on their rusty bikes with wonky wheels. No, they were lycra-clad stormtroopers with fixed faces, insect skull helmets and shaved muscular legs. I kept to the side of the path to avoid them. Sometimes the cyclists were interspersed with roller-bladders, skateboarders and several people on wheeled wind-surfing boards who flew past at a tremendous speed. I was the slowest moving human being in the nature reserve, it seemed.

When I emerged at the southern end of the reserve I stood beside a small lake and considered my options. It was late afternoon and although the landscape was lit up with strong yellow light from the western sun, the eastern sky was contrastingly dark and broody. Perhaps there would be a storm, I thought. Ahead of me the path rose up to meet the curving seawall that had been built by the unemployed after the war. The works were impressive and the entire lower western part of the island had been reclaimed from the sea with nothing more than picks and shovels. Now, over seventy years later, it was mostly salt marshes and birch forests. The soil was thin, chalky and full of flints, and a local urban myth said there were land mines buried here. Skull and crossbones signs proclaiming *Keep Out - Danger,* chased from my mind any thoughts of camping in those birch woods.

The cyclists, wind surfers and roller-bladers were still whizzing by every other minute or so and I felt that if I stood around much longer I might end up entangled with one of them in a messy heap on the ground. Should I head south and camp on the beach or should I veer off and put my tent up in an old oak forest just outside the reserve? Turning around I could just make out the now-distant towers of Copenhagen to the north. I was far enough away from the city to feel that I was escaping its gravitational pull, yet at the same time I had an uneasy feeling about my situation.

It's precisely these half-wild buffer areas around major cities where some of the darkest happenings occur, and this part of the island was no exception. A serial killer had roamed here in the late 1980s when my wife was a teen-ager, his reign of terror lasting for years. This, and other evil happenings, lingered on in the minds of Copenhagen-ers and, indeed, the lake by which I was now stood would be familiar to fans of the Danish noir TV series *The Killing* as the location where a car was dredged up. What's more, Kongelunden, where I was considering pitching my tent, was the setting for the opening scene in which a young girl is brutally murdered.

All things considered, I opted to head to the beach. It was only about a quarter of an hour's walk away and I knew it to be a more or less deserted strand of crispy black sea-weed. Somewhat flyblown, at least it would be peaceful. Or so I thought. I could see the kite surfers from some distance as I trudged towards the beach, aching to put down my heavy pack. When I reached the shore there must have been a hundred of them. I sat down by my pack and watched them.

They stood on boards that sliced across the surface of the sea, propelled by the force of the wind in the sails to which they were attached. It seemed amazing to me that so many of them could be in action together without getting their strings entangled. Yet they moved with sublime grace, us-ing nothing more than the energy freely provided by the elements to execute their spins, grabs and loops. Like hu-man pendulums they moved hypnotically, swinging back and forth across the choppy grey waters beneath the dark-ening sky. One might have thought that such acrobatics would be enacted with playful yelps of joy, but in fact si-lence reined over the scene. Only the slight plop of the boards hitting the water and the hum of the wind on the taut ropes could be heard and I was reminded of one of those 'silent raves' I had seen, where people dance wearing wireless headphones that deliver the same music synchron-ically to all. The faces of the surfers – men and women – were fixed in the same expressions as the cyclists: deadpan and serious.

Maybe this was the latest trend, something to be 'into' to fill in the gaps between bouts of work, or to constitute a part of one's keep fit regime. As such it seemed like an enactment of something sad, like a piece of performance art that was supposed to represent collective tragedy and alienation. Atomised people having fun in the same place but not together.

I took out my diary and wrote some more words to add to those I had scribbled down earlier.

Walked out across Amager Fælled with the sun slanting down out of the west and dark thunderous clouds moving in from the east. Colours of the wildflowers and hedgerows illuminated nicely. So much to forage along the way! I have already eaten handfuls of sea buckthorn berries, a few hazel nuts and some damsons. I have my tree eyes in now. Last time I was here they were just 'trees' – a kind of green background fuzz – but now they are hawthorn, birch, alder, elder, hazel, dog rose, sea blackthorn, willow and mountain ash. Knowing their names and which parts are edible makes the world more interesting, somehow.

Feeling a bit anxious, like I'm doing something subversive. I stick out like a sore thumb with my sleeping bag and my staff. Perhaps I should have trimmed the beard a bit before I left and covered the gash on my leg. Nobody yet has smiled or said 'hello' to me – but then I remember this is the way here. Will I last out? My pack is very heavy, I must have brought too much food. I'm looking forward to to-night and I hope it rains. I wonder if I will be left in peace here. Yesterday, I went for a drink at Cafe Bizarro with Wes and Anna and their baby. Wes said "Watch out for the wild animals". But it's not the four-legged animals I'm worried about, it's the two-legged ones.

Headlines as I left: "And so it begins: Ukraine destroys Russia Convoy". That and Robin Williams hanging him-self.

Chapter 4. A call to adventure

"Forget safety. Live where you fear to live. Destroy your reputation. Be notorious!"

– Rumi

The oak forest of Kongelund – the King's Forest – lay only slightly inland from where I was standing on the beach. Walking over to it I put my pack down beside a wooden bench at a municipal picnic spot by the gate that led into the nature reserve. From my pack I got out some rye bread and a tub of spreadable cheese containing flecks of prawn meat. I spread it on with my lightweight plastic knife and drank some water. As I ate I wondered where to put the tent for my first night. There was a fire pit here, as well as a wooden table, but I figured these features would likely attract teenagers after dark. Still, I reasoned, it was a Sunday so maybe Amager's youth would have done their partying over the previous two nights. I mulled this over before deciding to put up the tent in a thicket of black alder saplings behind a cluster of bigger trees. I would be mostly out of sight there, I figured, and fully out of sight when darkness fell.

My plan was to spend only a single night here and be off again at first light. It would give me a chance to test the tent, which my brother-in-law had given me as an offcast. It was remarkably easy to put up and only took a couple of minutes. When I had done so I sat in it and looked out from my secret vantage point. A few minutes passed and a family on bikes came and sat at the table in the picnic area. Their two young children immediately spotted my little blue tent behind the trees and came over to gawp at me until their father pulled them away again.

A plane flew overhead, its landing gear down, ready to hit the tarmac. Despite my sylvan setting I was not far from the end of one of the runways at Copenhagen airport, which is Scandinavia's largest hub. The planes here were only a couple of hundred feet overhead, almost close enough to see the rivets on the fuselage. Past experience told me that there would be a plane either landing or taking off here every three or four minutes. I considered what I was doing here, sitting in a tent in a woodland at the end of a runway. There is, supposedly, a right in much of Scandinavia that permits camping anywhere. Called *allemansrätten* in Swedish – meaning 'every man's right', or more simply 'the right to roam' – this most liberal of laws gives anyone the right to camp anywhere for a night or two, as long as they don't cause any damage to crops or private property. I intended to make full use of this right on my journey.

On reflection, however, it did not occur to me at the time that I had never actually seen anyone *enacting* this right. Nevertheless, whatever my rights, the spot I had picked to camp on didn't seem right at all. It was half-visible to passers-by, and maybe being half-visible was worse than being fully visible. So I packed up again and leaped across a ditch to enter into the forest itself. It wasn't long before I found the perfect spot beneath an old oak tree about fifty metres into the woodland. I put up the tent again and cleared away all the fallen sticks in the surrounding area. When I had finished I sat down on a stump and looked at my new temporary home. It was perfect. There were dead sticks everywhere for a fire on which to cook my dinner and, being near the forest edge, enough light was getting through to allow a proliferation of forest flowers to grow. What's more, nobody would be able to see me here. And then I looked up.

High up in the tree an immense branch had been broken off and it was hanging there by the merest strip of bark. So fragile did it look it seemed as if the slightest gust of wind would cause it to fall and skewer me in my tent. That was no good. Perhaps it had been hanging there for years but there was no way I would get even a wink of sleep as long as I knew it was poised above me like the sword of Damocles. Wearily, I took down the tent again and dragged it over to another spot, this time in a small glade of saplings and flowers, and set up camp again. Third time lucky, I thought. By now it was early evening and I was wondering what to do to pass the time. I began to look around at the forest and take more notice of my surroundings. If I had been here a couple of years previously, before I owned and managed my own woodland, I would have considered it a pleasant enough setting. But since I had delved into the world of trees I had developed a deeper appreciation of all things sylvan and what might have seemed like 'just a bunch of trees' to me before, I was now able to appreciate in much more considered detail. And what my new tree eyes saw was not pretty.

The 300 year-old oaks were still, for the most part, standing, but in between them were planted row upon row of conifers. Many of these had already been harvested mechanically in blocks and it appeared that I had pitched my tent in an area that had been cut four or five years previously. To fell the trees giant pieces of forestry machinery had been used and the damage that it had inflicted was to be seen everywhere. Huge ruts in the ground betrayed where the wheels had rolled and the smaller trees, I now noticed, were all bent or broken and had clearly been crushed by the machines. And then I noticed the crowns of the great oaks had been damaged, sometimes quite considerably, presumably by the falling pines. No doubt that was what had caused the hanging branch in the tree I had pitched my tent underneath. Elsewhere there were trees sprayed with fluorescent paint, and others with huge bleeding dents and damage to their trunks. Nearby, on a forestry ride, hundreds of straight pine trunks had been stacked in piles.

The one positive aspect to all this devastation was the liberal amount of deadwood left lying around. I built up a small fire in a compression in the ground, first making sure to clear away any loose leaf litter and small twigs for, although the ground was wet from recent rains and the chance of a forest fire in Denmark was practically nil, I didn't want to take any chances. Soon the fire was crackling and burning. I scouted out the area, making sure that nobody could see me from any angle, and when I was satisfied this was the case I sat down on a tree stump and busied myself with chopping some branches with the axe. There was no sound except the crackle of my camp fire and the occasional roar of the planes coming in to land.

I tried to relax but I had a terribly uneasy feeling that I was being watched. I told myself I was just being paranoid and poured myself a nip of whisky from a small bottle I had picked up at the airport for just such an occasion. The transition from the comforts of city living to the uncertainties of camping in the half-wild was bound to be unnerving to some extent I told myself. I pulled out my diary and wrote a little.

There are hardly any birds in this forest – I've only seen one and heard none. Perhaps it's the roar of the planes overhead. But there are plenty of ash trees (I thought they were all supposed to have died?). It has an eerie feeling here and I'm not sure I like it. I have a longing to go up north as far as I can – up into the wilds of Sweden or Norway, north of the Polar Circle. I'm sure a train will take me there but will decide tomorrow morning what I am going to do. Just one night here and then I'm gone.

Writing here didn't feel right, so I put the pen down and took out a book to read. The book was Marcus Aurelius's *Meditations*. Aurelius had been a Roman emperor, but it seemed he had been a reluctant one. The pomp of state had bored him and he instead filled his head with philosophical musings on the meaning of life. He is regarded as one of the later Stoics, and I had considered that he might have something to teach us in this modern age. The Stoics, above all, explored the themes of virtue, happiness and free will, and I had an innate feeling that such considerations would be of use to us in the years and decades ahead.

I began to read Marcus Aurelius but my mind couldn't latch onto the words. Perhaps it was the Penguin Modern Classics cover, which always managed to instil a fear of 'literature' in me. I put the book down and rummaged around for the other one I had brought along. Two books, I had decided, was my limit. My pack was already too heavy and books were something of an indulgence. In fact, I had three books if you included the red notebook that was my diary. The other book was entitled '*Soulcraft: Crossing into the Mysteries of Nature and Psyche*', written by the American author Bill Plotkin. A picture of him on the dust cover showed a tanned and healthy man much younger looking than his years.

The book had been recommended to me by someone who had read my blog and I had slung it into my pack without even reading the back cover. It wasn't the usual type of book I would read. A quick flick through it raised the suspicion that it might be full of psychobabble. Mr Plotkin looked like the kind of open-hearted Californian who is anathema to the stodgy and conservative British upbringing to which I had been subjected. I wasn't sure why it had been recommended to me but seeing as I was on a journey in search of some answers I decided to indulge Mr Plotkin. I flipped it open and began to read.

"Contemporary society has lost touch with soul and the path to psychological and spiritual maturity, or true adulthood. Instead we are encouraged to create lives of predictable security, false normality, material comfort, bland entertainment, and the illusion of eternal youth. Most of our leaders – political, cultural and economic – represent and defend a non-sustainable way of life built upon military aggression, the control and exploitation of nature's 'resources' and an entitled sense of national security that ignores the needs of other species, other nations, tribes and races, and our own future generations. These values

do not reflect our deeper human nature.

"Successful navigation of this most perilous time in human history requires psychologically and spiritually mature men and women who can engender a mature human species."

After reading only the first few pages I knew it was going to be one of *those* books. What I mean by this is that there are only a handful of books that I have read in my life which have spoken to me so directly at exactly the point in time when I needed to read them – and this looked like one of them. I continued to read. Bill Plotkin described an incident in his early years as an adult when he had climbed a mountain peak and, upon reaching the summit and gazing out across the vast expanse of snow-capped mountains stretching to the horizon, had experienced a force so powerful that he felt like a portal to another world had been suddenly flung open. Upon returning to civilisation he immediately abandoned the safe career for which he had worked so hard, and set off on a journey into the depths of wild nature. He writes:

"Our society is forever erecting barriers between its citizens and the inner/outer wilderness. On the outer side, we have our air-conditioned houses and automobiles, gated communities and indoor malls, fences and animal control officers, dams and virtual realities. On the inner side we're offered prescribed mood enhancers, alcohol, and street drugs; consumerism and dozens of other soul-numbing addictions; fundamentalism, transcendentalism and other escapisms; rigid belief systems as to what is good and what is bad and teachings that God or some other paternal figure will watch over us and protect our delicate lives.

"But when we escape beyond these artificial barriers, we discover something astonishing: nature and soul not only depend on each other, long for each other and are in the end of the same substance, like twins or trees sharing the same roots."

What, it seems, he experienced on top of that mountain was a sudden realisation that he had a greater purpose in life, and that purpose was revealed to him by a voice that spoke to his soul. He continues:

"But, upon reaching the summit, my understanding of life changed and my adolescent trance ended. Lost in a sea of white peaks, I was pierced by an unfathomable sadness for a loss that was at once mine and not mine, and a hope for something bigger than I knew to hope for... Then the truth exploded into my awareness. I heard myself gasp. There was no denying it: my university tenure track was a spiritual dead end and I simply had to leave, despite my promising career, despite the inevitable incomprehension from family and colleagues, despite my not knowing where I would go, how I would survive or who I would be."

I was enthralled.

"The journey of descent begins with a call to adventure, a stirring declaration from the depths, from the gods and goddesses, that it is time to leave behind everything you thought your life was supposed to be."

At the height of this epiphany a voice had spoken to him. The voice had told him that he should build cocoons. *"Build cocoons?"*, he thought. Whatever could that mean? Its meaning was revealed to him over time, he wrote. His duty was to help people build their own cocoons; to enable them, like caterpillars, to radically transform themselves into new beings. This, he concludes, has been his life's true work, and now, decades later, he was able to reflect on its value. He finishes the chapter by writing:

"I have had the privilege of accompanying thousands of people... as they enter life-changing thresholds: endings, beginnings, crossroads, upheavals, crises and periods of emptiness or healing... It's not too late for you no matter how tired or sceptical you might be. And it's as natural as being born or dying, as natural as a snake shedding its skin, a tree dropping its leaves, a thundercloud releasing

rain… or caterpillar forming its cocoon."

I closed the book and put it down, my mind now alive to the possibilities that lay ahead. I had set out on this journey with Einstein's famous adage at the forefront of my mind, but with no idea of how to grapple with it:

We can't solve our problems using the same kind of thinking we used when we created them.

But now it seemed like I had a guide on my journey. I wanted to sit there and read the rest of the book right there, even if it took all night. In my excitement any anxiety had evaporated and, having been completely absorbed by the book I noticed that I had let the fire die down. The thin wisps of smoke rose lazily upwards and hung in the still air of the clearing and I realised then that the planes had stopped flying overhead and the distant voices of the Sunday strollers had gone. Everything was still and quiet and the sun slanted down into my little clearing, falling on a single long-stemmed wildflower beside the entrance to my tent. The flower seemed to be moving slightly, despite there being no wind. I gazed at it in curiosity.

And then I saw it.

Now, friends will sometimes tell me that I have a love of embellishing tales. After all, I reason, if a tale is worth telling then it's worth spicing up with all the little bardic details that make its telling all the more memorable, isn't it? But what I saw right then needed no embellishment and made me freeze to the spot, my breath suddenly stuck in my throat. For there, clinging to the top of the sunlit flower's stem, was the largest caterpillar I had ever seen in my life.

And it was staring right at me.

I muttered something incredulously and stood up. As I did so its face followed my movement. I walked over and bent down to have a look at it and it looked right back at me. It was perhaps five inches long, as thick as a slug, and it had a patterned face that looked like a cartoon Chinese Zen master chewing something bitter. I had no idea that caterpillars could grow so large. As I moved to one side it followed me again with its whole head. Another gasp. I would scarcely have been more amazed had it started blowing smoke rings and talking about Alice. For a moment I actually did expect it to start blowing smoke rings and talking about Alice.

I felt I should address it, but it seemed a bit strange talking to a caterpillar in a forest. I managed a hesitant "Well, hello, look at you", and it continued to stare at me as if *I* were the strange interloper in this scene, which, on reflection, I probably was. Instead I took out my camera and took a few close-up pictures of it. I checked the images on the screen display of the camera, just to make sure they were real and I wasn't dreaming. Then I took a couple more, and the caterpillar didn't seem to like it and raised a few legs to indicate its displeasure. I spent several minutes in this strange state of wonder, puzzling what this could mean and experiencing a mix of confusion, humour and vague anxiety.

The thought occurred to me that perhaps the creature had fallen from the fuselage of one of the planes coming in to land – a plane that was returning from some colourful land where caterpillars grew to such sizes. Who knows, I thought, maybe there were all sorts of exotic hitchhikers in these woods. Could there be a rational explanation, such as coincidence? After all, I had literally just finished reading about caterpillars being heralds for new journeys and experiences, and here I was talking to a giant one. I didn't have long to dwell on these thoughts because all of a sudden there was the sound of a car's engine and a few moments later a shaven head was bobbing towards me through the undergrowth at a considerable clip. A uniformed man burst through the bushes and came marching towards me with an officious look on his face. Yep, I was being busted.

"What the hell are you doing?", he barked, stomping into the clearing. "Camping is not permitted in this area. You could burn down the whole forest!". He looked down at my small fire, which was smouldering weakly, perhaps wondering whether he should smother it.

I played dumb, pretending not to understand him. "I was told I could camp here", I protested, a bit weakly. He sized me up for a moment, and seemed to decide that I didn't represent a threat. "No, you may not camp here", he continued, a bit more softly and in English.

"Did you not see the QE code on the gate?" I blinked at him in incomprehension. He continued, "If you had you could have downloaded the app and it would tell you where the permitted camping zone is located".

I apologised that I hadn't. In any case, I thought, who'd ever heard of a forest that you needed a smartphone app to understand? "If we let people camp anywhere they want then they would do damage to the forest", he went on, although to me it looked like they were doing a good job of damaging the forest without the campers. "And it is dangerous for you because the noise from the planes could damage your hearing."

I reassured him my hearing was unlikely to be permanently damaged by the occasional aircraft flying overhead, although it did occur to me that perhaps I was a potential security threat and I wondered how he had been so easily able to locate me. I thought perhaps there might be hidden cameras in the trees.

And then the second unusual thing in the space of two minutes occurred. The park ranger seemed to be giving me a strange look, as if a thought were dawning within him. I had a peculiar feeling too… it was as if I had met this man somewhere before in entirely different circumstances. And then I realised that this was indeed the case, that I had bought an antique pine chest off him two years before, a chest that now rested at the foot of my bed in Cornwall a thousand miles away. I recalled him saying at the time that he worked as a forest ranger when I visited him at his old farmhouse with its cobbled courtyard and I had joked to my wife that I didn't think there were any forest rangers in Denmark and that he must have been making it up. The feeling was like that of being in a dream in which one person morphs into another. In dreams this tends to feel perfectly natural but in this case it seemed far from natural, this chance meeting of someone I half-knew on the outskirts of a city of over half a million people.

"You don't live here?", he asked with a hint of curiosity in his voice. No, I replied, I was just visiting and was planning to go to Sweden in the morning. I had no desire to remind him of our previous meeting. His eyes narrowed a little as he looked at me – maybe he recognised me as well but thought better of saying so – and then he turned away and was off.

"I will let you stay here tonight but you must be gone by tomorrow", he called out over his shoulder as he made his way back to the ride where his utility vehicle was parked. "But don't light any more fires."

After the sound of his engine died away silence returned once more to the glade. I breathed a sigh of relief and piled a few more sticks on the fire. The caterpillar was still staring at me expectantly. "What are you looking at?", I said, sitting down on a stump and prodding the fire. I felt closed in, as though I was being watched at every step. I didn't know where I was going the next day, but I had a strong feeling that I wanted to head north. The lakes and forests north of Stockholm would be good – the mountain-studded wilderness north of the Arctic Circle would be even better. I yearned for the wild, to rediscover the voice that it spoke with, to rejoin the conversation once more.

But it wasn't to be. There would be no Arctic Circle or mountains, although I didn't know it yet.

41

Chapter 5. Means of escape

"You're off to great places,
Today is your day,
Your mountain is waiting,
So get on your way!"

– Dr. Seuss

The next day I awoke early. During the night a gentle rain had fallen but there had been no storm. I had gone to bed early, as soon as it got dark, but was awoken later by the sound of motor scooters and raised voices. What seemed like hours of teenage revelry and shouting had ensued, followed by the sound of bottles being smashed against rocks. But then the rain had come and the teenagers had gone away again. I was thankful that I had had the foresight to move my tent from its original position next to the picnic tables and fire pit, which was now littered with broken glass, empty beer cans and the fluttering detritus of fast food wrappers.

I packed up the tent as the gentle patter of rain fell around me. There can be few things more soothing than peacefully falling rain at the end of a hot summer. Each raindrop heralds the death of summer's sweet exuberance, and it is received gratefully by the soil, which in response emits a decadent and satisfying aroma by way of thanks. The caterpillar was still there but it was not moving now. It had fitted its body to the curve of the upper part of the flower's stem and appeared to be sleeping. Perhaps it was getting ready to make a cocoon. I bade it farewell and set off, having covered the ash in the fire pit with a spread of damp leaves.

I walked out of the wood and towards the shore. In the distance the city hummed as Monday morning commuters poured in from the suburbs by car, train, bus and bike. Not too long ago I would have been one of them and, indeed, if you look at a particular arterial road using Google Street View and if you know what you are looking for you will see a black-clad faceless figure riding a black bicycle among other faceless figures. That's me. It felt strangely appropriate to have become nothing more than a digital ghost on the canvas of this ephemeral sea-level city.

I walked through the grey drizzle towards a place where I knew I could catch a bus. It was situated on the outskirts of the wood beside a residential unit for refugees. Walking parallel to the shore I could see the car park in the distance and watched as a Mercedes drove slowly towards me with lights on and window wipers going. Two figures were within, watching me approach, and as I neared a door opened and a young woman got out.

"Where are the kite surfers?" she called to me.

"You've missed them", I said. "They were here yesterday but they've left now."

She looked despondent and got back in the Mercedes without a word. After a moment they drove off, leaving me plodding along in their wake with my too-heavy backpack. I stopped and got out my plastic poncho, putting it on over my head so that it covered all of me including my pack. I continued walking towards the refugee centre hidden among the trees, wondering why a girl would turn up look-ing for kite surfers so early on a rainy Monday morning. I still had my staff in my hand and I paused to look at my reflection in a puddle that had formed in a pothole. In the dark green poncho with its bulbous hood and with my staff in hand I looked like a fantasy wizard, or maybe a pilgrim. I chuckled at my reflection as flecks of rain birthed tiny circles in the muddy image.

Outside the refugee centre I waited for the bus to take me to the airport. I could see, looking at the timetable, that I had just missed one and the next would not be along for another hour. I sighed and pushed my pack under a hedge to keep the worst of the rain off it. The refugee centre was a barracks type affair with an open gate that allowed those inside to come and go as they pleased. Its presence was incongruous in this woodland setting and seemed accidentally placed. It was utterly silent and appeared lifeless, but I knew that within it there were families from the Middle East and Africa, flung here to this peaceful hamlet on the edge of a damp wood by events outside their control.

I leaned against a lamp post and read my book. At the correct time – not a minute too soon or late – the bus arrived to take me to the airport. As it pulled up at the bus stop a door opened in the refugee centre and about a dozen Africans, mostly women with children, rushed out and got on board. The bus swung around the car park and soon we were back in the dreary suburbs, amongst the serried ranks of modest houses with modest gardens, the pizza joints, convenience stores and dog grooming parlours. The bus slowly filled up with commuters heading to work.

I listened to the women from the centre, who were speaking a mixture of English and their own language. One of them, a tidy-looking young woman with an open face, had a small inquisitive boy of about four. Evidently he was bored and decided it would be fun to stand up in the centre isle and practice balancing as the bus went around corners. His mother, distractedly at first, told him to sit down. He ignored her and she carried on with her conversation with an older woman. On about the third order for him to sit down she turned fierce and, reaching out, grabbed him by the ear and pulled him back to his seat. He screamed out and she belted him across the face with the back of her hand, hard enough to knock him sideways onto the seat.

The other passengers on the bus, disconnected in their own virtual electronic worlds, pretended not to notice, even though hitting a child is a criminal offence in Denmark. The boy, whimpering, slunk away and sat in the seat behind me. Shiny, orb-like tears rolled down his cheeks and after a while he leaned forward and said in a husky emotion-choked voice "She's a bad mamma, my mamma." I didn't know what to say to him.

The airport was busy on this Monday morning. Besuited men and women strode purposefully between check-in desks on their way to meetings in Brussels, London and Frankfurt. I had only a few hundred kroner in my wallet, barely enough to survive for a couple of days in this expensive part of the world. I found an ATM and put my card in. My plan was to withdraw a few thousand kroner, which would be enough to pay for train fares, food and the occasional bed and breakfast if need be. But the ATM had other ideas.

Request denied. Insufficient funds.

A cold chill went through me. I tried a lower amount and got the same message. On the third attempt I heard the reassuring sound of money being counted inside the machine. It spat out a thin wad of notes and returned my card. I sighed and put the money in my wallet. This money would have to last me for almost two weeks. I shook my head and felt a weight of gloom settle on me. How would I survive on so little money, I asked myself.

I was hungry and needed a coffee so I went into a 7-11 and ordered Danish pastries (confusingly called Vienna pastries in Denmark) and a paper cup of milky coffee. Here I sat for some time, watching as people scurried past like clockwork mice. It was almost hypnotic watching them stream past, all of them with somewhere to go and something to do. A familiar face sailed past in the moving crowd, a Latin-looking woman wearing a smart uniform. I recognised her as an old friend, a graphic designer who illustrated children's books and who had worked at the newspaper on the layout desk. I could have told you that she was from Bolivia, that her husband was a maker of independent films, that she hated the long cold Danish winters and that to earn some extra income she greeted groups of Spanish tourists at the airport. I called out to this familiar face but she was already gone, dissolving in the crowd. Once more, I felt like a ghost in this city.

Delving in my pack I pulled out my mobile phone. I connected up to the free airport wi-fi and called my wife on Skype. She asked me if I was enjoying myself. Having children had meant that it had been over a decade since I had had the chance to wander alone. I told her that two evenings before I had gone out into the city to meet some friends, and how they hadn't turned up and I had ended up sitting in a bar trying to speak to some American tourists who only wanted to tell me how expensive everything was and how much cheaper it was back home. I told her about getting ejected from the shopping mall and getting in trouble with the forest ranger. It's raining and I have almost no money, I said. Oh, and I set off your mother's fire alarm by mistake, I added. My wife was back in Cornwall, working long days and nights caring for the old and the sick, and here was I, in her country, complaining about feeling lonely.

"You're a barrel of laughs, aren't you?" she replied.

"Sorry."

"Where are you going?" she asked.

"Sweden", I replied. "Maybe up past the Polar Circle. If I can afford it – I have hardly any money left."

"Just look after yourself", she replied. "And try to cheer up – I wish I was in your shoes instead of working all these hours for peanuts."

"I'm sorry", I said. "I'll give you a call when I'm back in civilisation."

Hanging up, I placed the phone back in my pack. The battery was almost dead and I didn't have a charger. That was all part of the plan. I wanted to escape from the ubiquitous electronic interference that has come to dominate our lives. If nobody knew where I was or how they could contact me then that was for the best as far as I was concerned. Cloud hidden, whereabouts unknown, as the Zen saying has it. I stood up to leave, finishing the last of my coffee and wiping some pastry flakes away.

A man wearing a business suit appeared at my side and enquired if I was leaving and whether he could take my seat. I affirmed that this was so and he sat down quickly, placing his coffee and a copy of the newspaper he had just bought at the kiosk on the table before him. It was my old newspaper – so familiar to me and yet so alien-looking. I had moved on and it was still here: at least some things never change. I hitched my pack onto my back and picked up the staff from where it had been leaning against a refrigeration cabinet for bottles of Coke. Ghosts are never welcome and it was time to move on. I had twelve clear days before me, no kids to look after, no pressing work that needed doing, no commitments to speak of, no connection to the electronic cloud and no real idea of where I was going.

This was my secret as I threaded my way through the busy stream of air passengers and descended the steps to the subterranean railway station.

Chapter 6. Malmö

"If the path before you is clear, you're probably on someone else's."

– Joseph Campbell

The train sped across the bridge above the steely grey waters of the Øresund – the stretch of water separating Denmark and Sweden. The monochrome blur of Malmö came closer, flashing as if it were a cinematic frame animation as we passed the steel supports of this immense bridge. Taking place around me was a scene of some liveliness. I was sitting in the midst of a great family group of mothers, aunts and children of all ages who were leaping around in excitement and taking pictures of one-another with their mobile phones. The mothers all wore *hijabs* and had piles of shopping bags arrayed around their feet. Everyone was shouting to one another in a mixture of Arabic and English.

It was all very un-Scandinavian, an effect amplified by the fact that there were no European faces apart from my own on this particular carriage. A little girl, not much older than a toddler, clambered up on my knee and used it as a platform from which to view the foamy waves speeding past below. "Abba, Abba!" she cried out, pointing at the Swedish shore and jabbing a finger against the rain-streaked window. Momentarily, I was perplexed. Abba? Then I remembered that *abba* means 'daddy' in Arabic – perhaps this little girl's father was living there. It was a comedy moment.

Soon we were easing over Swedish land and the train's braking system gradually slowed our approach to the main train station in Malmö. My flock of fellow passengers left the train, as did I, and headed out into the rainy city streets. I stayed within the station and, leaning my pack against a wall, pondered my next move. I paused to take in the subtle energies that one can sense when moving from one country to the next. Sweden, as ever, felt like it had a slightly more empty and echoey feel to it than Denmark.

One can immediately feel one is in a large country, although I'm not sure how. To me at least, all of Scandinavia has an old and slightly frigid feel to it. Sensations of cold mountain rock and empty caves filled with icy water pervade the senses. It feels like a place battling darkness, and maybe that's why Scandinavians love to celebrate the light, with their bubbly pop music, their fondness for the festival of Santa Lucia, in the dark period just before winter solstice, and their white-walled apartments and obsession with tea lights. Perhaps there is a deep recognition, unspoken, that life is a constant struggle for light, that if the guard were to slip then darkness would soon seep back in. And, deeper still, there is a feeling of an ancient and unassimilated culture, like something trapped under ice and waiting for the thaw. I feel an echo of sadness, a yearning of sorts that can be enchanting or can be depressing, depending on how it is received.

Malmö lies at one end of the line for Sweden. Most of the action in this long and sparse nation of less than ten million souls concentrates around the central region of Stockholm. Twice as many people live in and around London than in the whole of this echoing country. I looked at the train departure signs for clues as to where I should go. Stockholm would seem the obvious first choice, and I even had friends there who might be willing to put me up for a night or two before heading further north. I wandered over to a ticket machine and punched in my destination. When the price came up I almost gasped – this was more than double the amount I had allocated for the whole trip. Suddenly the prospect of getting to the far north seemed less realistic. I punched in a few other distant destinations, but all of them were beyond my means.

I retreated to a plastic bench and considered my options. If anyone had an idea how I could get north, I figured, it would be the tourist information office. I craved vast expanses of wilderness, and imagined pitching my tent on a lonely bluff, awakening to the sun rising over immense vistas of mountains, glaciated valleys and dark green forests. Perhaps they would be able to tell me how I could make this yearning a reality. I followed the signs in the station and headed outside to the office over the road, pulling my cap down over my eyes to stop the rain getting on my glasses.

But my romantic dream of escape was quickly drowned in the bathtub of reality by the sanguine lady behind the desk. With her grey hair done up in a bun and half moon glasses perched on her nose she was like a school headmistress, and she had sternness down to a tee. "The Arctic Circle?" she asked incredulously. "It's as far away as Rome – what makes you think such a journey should be cheap?"

"I don't know", I sputtered. "Isn't there some way I could get there on a budget?" She studied me as the word 'budget' hung in the air. I clearly wasn't the kind of highly liquid tourist she had no doubt been trained to welcome to her country.

"What is it exactly that you want?" she said carefully. Given my time and budget limitations there was no point being oblique with her so I outlined my vision of trying to escape. A kind of mini-break from modern civilisation was what I was after. I wanted somewhere wild, with animals and trees rather than golf courses and holiday homes, and where I could camp and be undisturbed. And that I could afford to get to without taking out a loan.

"I see", she said, pursing her lips. "Are you a naturist?"

"A naturist? I don't think so", I said, although the idea of walking around with no clothes on didn't seem that tempting in the current weather. "But I'm not interested in being around other people, naked or otherwise", I added.

She considered this for a moment and then got out a map

and unfolded it on the desk. It was a map of the entire region of Skåne, known in English as Scania, the southern region of Sweden in which I now stood. "Here", she said, circling a dark green blob with a red pen, "is where you will find what you are looking for". I looked closer. It was a national park, not a very big one, and it was not very far from Malmö. She explained. "Söderåsens National Park is a – how do you say? – a crack, yes a crack in the surface of the planet. It is very beautiful in this place. Here you will find ancient forests and there are places where you can stay for free. There is a lake called after our god Odin and you can swim in it and there is a place where you can take pictures of the view too." She looked at me for approval.

It wasn't what I had envisioned, seeming far too close to where I was standing now. "In this place you can put up your tent, if that is what you wish." She fished around and pulled out some brochures showing pictures of the park. It really did look beautiful though, with sweeping vistas of forests in autumnal glory, and pictures of flowing rivers and colourful birds.

"So I can just camp where I want?", I asked.

"Absolutely not!", she replied hastily. "You may have heard about our *allemansrätt* but you must follow our rules and not break them." I wasn't too sure what she meant by this so asked her to qualify it, that it had been my understanding you could camp anywhere as long as you didn't cause damage.

"No", she hooted, arching her eyebrows as though I'd suggested something improper. "You can not do this! Think what would happen if people could just camp where they wanted!". I was a little miffed by her reaction but consoled myself that I'd gauge the situation when I reached the national park, if that's where I was headed. Perhaps it was only in the wild and bleak north where you could be truly free to roam, and not in these more densely-populated southern lowlands.

I thanked her for her help and left the tourist information office. As I crossed the road back to the train station I had mixed feelings about the place she had recommended. On the one hand I was deflated about letting go of the prospect of heading to the far north, but on the other it was appealing that I wouldn't have to travel too far and the pictures she had shown me certainly did appeal.

Inside I looked at the screen displaying the trains waiting to head north and a bad thought flickered across my mind. What if I were to stow aboard one? To hide in the bathroom, or pretend I had lost my ticket if caught? Perhaps it was worth a shot. After my two brushes with authority the previous day I already felt like something of an outlaw, so why not go the whole hog and become a stowaway? But the thought didn't last long. I would almost certainly be caught and ejected, possibly even arrested. And it was at least a two day journey to get to the north. It wasn't worth the risk, I decided.

I went for a short walk around the centre of Malmö to think things over. A funfair was on, but it didn't look much fun and the ride operators huddled from the rain and sucked on cigarettes. I paused by a bridge over a canal and looked down into the water at a sculpture of a troll. I felt completely at a loss, unsure what to do with myself or where I should go. Hunger stirred again and I returned to the railway station. Inside I followed the icon that depicted a person eating and found myself in a small food court offering lobster, smoked salmon and caviar. A waiter approached with a menu and I backed out of the door, apologising.

Around the corner was a Max Hamburger – Sweden's own version of McDonald's – offering food at prices I could more readily afford. I queued up and purchased a giant burger dripping with cheese and bacon and surrounded by fries. The girl who served me placed a receipt on my plastic tray saying that my consumption of the burger had contributed 3.3kg of carbon to the global atmosphere.

"Enjoy your meal", she said, flashing a smile.

I took the food over to a table and sank my teeth into the huge burger. It was heavenly. Meat, cheese and grease melted in my mouth and I ate it hungrily, shoving in french fries dipped in mayonnaise and drinking the large cup of cola that came with it. I devoured the entire thing in a matter of minutes and sat there slurping the last icy dregs of the drink with a straw. It had been years since I had eaten anything like this and all of a sudden I had a hunger for more. I went over and ordered another cheeseburger, wolfing it down in the same manner as the first one. After all, I reasoned, I didn't know where my next meal would be coming from.

Fortified by the junk food I rose to my feet and went over to purchase a bus ticket to take me to the national park. The woman behind the counter had not heard of Söderåsens National Park and I had to show her the map I had been given earlier. As I pointed at it I tried to pronounce the place names but she just frowned and looked more closely at the map. For a couple of minutes she consulted her computer screen and then issued me with a ticket that was clearly to the wrong place. I asked her to cancel it and she did so with an air of resignation. Behind me I could sense the people lining up to buy tickets growing impatient with me and my map. After a couple more minutes, during which time the woman consulted an equally nonplussed colleague, she returned the map to me and apologetically told me to go back to the tourist bureau and ask them for more precise information about where exactly on the bus network I should get a ticket to.

I left the station once more to cross the road to the tourism office. Inside a gaggle of Spanish tourists had filled the office and the staff were chatting away to them in fluent Spanish as though they were old friends. It looked like I would have a long wait before it was my turn to be served. Outside it had stopped raining and I felt full of energy after the burger and, on an impulse, instead of wasting my time figuring out buses and trains, I decided there and then to simply walk to Söderåsen. According to my map it was about 60km, and I figured I could cover half of that in a day with my pack on. In any case, the old university town of Lund was less than 20km away, so I would make that my first port of call.

I set out through the streets of Malmö, heading first through the centre with its wide boulevards and open squares, and then north out of the city alongside a main road. A heavy grey pall hung in the sky, threatening rain at any minute, and so I walked quickly in the hope that I could somehow outpace it. Within an hour I was out of the pleasant heart of Malmö and into the shabby post-industrial landscape around the northern zone of the city. Malmö had once been a place of manufacture but three decades of neglect and offshoring had left the city a rusty shell of its former self. A recent boom in services had brought in IT and biotech companies eager to hoover up the vacant lots and put up glass and steel blocks. As I walked through this ghostly post-modern urban landscape the spectre of Scandinavia's tallest building, the *Turning Torso* – shaped like a titanic cheese grater looking over its shoulder – hove in and out of view through the mist.

Malmö gets a bad press from some quarters, occasionally being called the most dangerous city in northern Europe. Others, usually those with an axe to grind, claim that the high number of Muslims living in the city have instituted their own sharia law. I knew such claims to be exaggerations and had seen time and again during my years living in Scandinavia that its cities are often used as a mental projection screen for various idealogical fantasies. Nevertheless, the city does have an uncomfortable reputation for randomly placed bombs and violent gun crime, the most recent episode of note involving a man named Peter Mangs, who had gone on a shooting spree over several months armed with a Glock handgun. Mangs would roam around the suburbs randomly killing people of non-ethnic Swedish identity and, after he was caught, he was suspected of 15 shootings and convicted for two murders. As ever, the dark side of Scandinavia contrasts sharply with the popular idyllic conviction many have about the peninsula, making for a lively topic of conversation and a source of dependable revenue for writers of Scandinavian noir.

After a couple of hours of winding my way through this landscape I was tired and so rested by a brick wall in a supermarket car park. I took out a little food and washed it down with some water. Filthy, ragged strips of cloud continued to scud past overhead and I wondered whether I would make it to Lund without getting drenched. I shouldered my pack again, determined to make it there before the evening. By way of self-bargaining I had decided to find a cheap hotel in which to enjoy a final night of comfort before heading out into the forest.

It took me the rest of the day to cover the distance between Malmö and Lund. The walk was at times dispiriting and slow. I trudged beside busy roads, over railway tracks and alongside muddy fields. Inevitably, the clouds finally burst, bucketing down on me as I sluiced my way through the long grass beside the roads. Someone threw a paper cup at me from a car, but missed. At one point, waiting for the barriers at a crossing, a train passed me by and I caught a glimpse of a blond woman looking out from behind a raindrop streaked window. Although I only glimpsed her face for an instant my mind associated her with Abba's Agnetha Fältskog in the video for the track *The Day Before You Came.* For the rest of the day I couldn't get the song out of my head.

Along the way I passed by abandoned factories with their windows broken and walls sprayed with graffiti. I could have been in Newcastle or Glasgow. People often forget, or at least overlook, the fact that Sweden and Norway still have a lot of heavy industry, as well as their own rust belts. The immense wilderness areas and coastal zones that each country possesses are home to mines, steelworks and – in Norway's case – one of the world's largest oil industries.

These extractive sectors bolster Scandinavia's balance of trade and provide a high standard of living to its relatively few citizens. It's not all windmills and bike lanes.

But Lund, as I knew from previous visits, was a far cry from the dark satanic mills of Sweden's hinterlands. A university town with a medieval centre, this compact city had been the place our family would sometimes visit in winter to sit indoors at a cafe and drink cappuccinos and eat pastries. In summer it was a place of honey-coloured cob cottages with nodding hollyhocks shedding their petals onto sun-warmed cobble stones. Winter turned it into a town of lights twinkling behind frosted windows and fur-clad people sipping hot chocolate in patisseries.

Memories of my kids, giddy with excitement, sliding splay-legged on the frozen puddles at the botanic gardens came back to me as I traipsed over the bypasses and to-wards the cathedral's twin towers. I walked the final approach into the town along bike lanes and, as evening drew near, through some well tended gardens. Allotment gardeners forked over the earth in the fading light and students ambled past me on their bicycles. It was a relief to see some human figures again as, for the entire day after setting out from Malmö, I had seen nobody unenclosed by a car or a train.

I was bone tired and my pack weighed me down like a stone. My neck ached. I had considered jettisoning some of the food but couldn't bear the thought of throwing it away, so instead I handed it over to a smartly dressed man sitting cross legged on the ground outside the train station. He was holding up a cardboard sign saying 'No home, no food' and thanked me as I handed over a carrier bag full of rice, pasta, instant coffee and some tins of food. He said he was from Syria when I asked him and he really did look like he had just stood up from a desk at his office job in Damascus and stepped straight onto this pavement in Sweden.

Unburdened slightly I walked over to the taxi rank and

asked the first driver in the line if he could take me to the cheapest motel in town. I felt too tired to walk the last mile or two, and I knew there was a cheap place to stay out towards the northern reaches of Lund. As I sat comfortably in the passenger seat and we accelerated out of the centre the driver was silent. I made some smalltalk to establish the fact that I was a foreigner. Past experience had taught me that this usually helped break the ice, and I wasn't wrong in this case. He said his name was Mohammed and that he was from Baghdad. He had come to Sweden a decade ago and had found the people icy to begin with but now he was getting used to it and said this was now his home. I asked why he had come to Sweden and he shot me a glance that was all I needed to know. "Blow up my house, my job, my family", he said. "Boom!", he concluded.

There wasn't much time to talk however, as we were soon at a large out-of-town shopping park bordered by concrete units, one of which was to be my lodgings for the night. Mohammed parked outside the entrance and fetched my backpack from the boot. "How much do I owe you?" I said, expecting it to be about 100 kroner. "Three hundred thirty", he said without a blink.

I was stunned. Surely it couldn't possibly be that much, since we had only come about two miles. He registered my surprise. "Sweden expensive", he grinned, producing a receipt from a small printer in the glove compartment which was wired up to a GPS satnav. "Here", he said, as proof.

I had no choice but to pay him and when I told the woman at the desk in the hotel she expressed shock and called out the other staff to relay in indignant tones what I just told her. "You must always take a white taxi", she told me earnestly, handing me a card with a taxi number on it. "Otherwise they will rip you off, or worse. The correct fee should be no more than 150 kroner." I went up to my room wondering what she had meant by a white taxi.

In my room I lay on the bed and rested my back for a while. I got up and looked out of the window. The view was so grim it was like a caricature of modern bleakness. There was a section of security fence, a portion of a grey pebble-dashed wall of a storage unit and a small strip of chemically manicured grass with a dead pigeon on it that lay on its back with its feet pointing skywards. By contrast, my room featured several framed pictures of awe-inspiring Swedish lakes surrounded by snow-frosted trees, perhaps to make up for the real view. I gazed at them and thought about that train ticket I couldn't afford.

Chapter 7. Live chickens and dead bishops

"The longest journey is the journey inward."

– Dag Hammarsköld

After a half hour of lying on the bed to rest my back I showered and changed into some clean clothes before leaving the motel and walking back into town. No taxi for me this time. It was a relief to move without the burden of my backpack and, as I walked along the pavements, I noticed that all the municipal hedgerows had been planted up with a great variety of fruit and berry producing bushes and shrubs. I couldn't help myself from stopping and picking a few of the ripest berries and seeds with a mind to take them back to my own woodland and nurture them into life. These lush and vibrant hedgerows contrasted sharply with the built urban environment around me and the anodyne shopping park I had just come from, with its neon signs and its oceanic parking lot.

At one point, to cross a busy road, I was forced to descend into an underpass. It was on the outskirts of another shopping precinct and the vehicles roared both above and around me as I emerged from below. I saw a group of five youths walking towards me. Loud and boisterous, as teenage boys often are, they were dressed in the style of American hoodlums. I shrank into myself doing my best to look as unworthy of interest as possible. The last thing I needed was to get entangled with a gang of delinquents. What happened next was, to say the least, unexpected, because as these youths were a few feet away from me, all swagger and sideways baseball caps, the most unusual thing happened.

A loud '*cockadoodledoo*' sounded and from a nearby bush

a cockerel suddenly darted out and stood there on the path between us. It raised its head again and emitted another cry and, it's probably fair to say, both the youths and I were equally as startled. They looked at the cock and then at me, and I looked at them and the cock cocked its head and looked at both me and at them at the same time. And then, all of a sudden, the youths started laughing. One of them grabbed for his mobile phone to film the spectacle. I moved slowly towards the rattled rooster in an attempt to stop it running out into the busy road.

"Is that yours?", one of the youths asked me in Swedish with a smirk. "No, is it yours?", I replied in English.

The youths looked at me as if I were an alien descended from another planet. "Is it yours?", repeated my inquisitor in an exaggerated plummy English accent, grinning sideways to his pals. They obliged his jibe, bursting into more gales of laughter. One of them upped him by addressing the cockerel and pointing at me: "Is it yours?". Further hilarity. He then positioned himself chest to chest with me and fist-bumped me as though we were old friends. I smiled wanly, wishing they would go away. The one doing the filming captured all of this on his phone and they huddled round to watch a repeat of all this comedy on the tiny screen, laughing like drains at the appropriate moment. I was worried that their next trick might be to chase the hapless bird out into the traffic and film its demise. But luckily for the cockerel they had had their fill of antics and carried on their way, swaggering off down into the underpass until all that remained of them were echoing voices and long shadows.

I bent down and tried to coax the cockerel towards me but instead it retreated further into the bush. I slowly moved some branches aside to reveal it. It was standing there with a small brown hen, protecting her defiantly, and they both looked at me with their chickeny eyes as if to say "What are you going to do to us?". I carefully moved back the branch and let them be. What were a pair of runaway chickens doing in the middle of a busy traffic intersection next to a shopping mall? And what was I supposed to do about it? I considered trying to catch them, but then what? They would probably just flee into the road and be run over. On the other hand I could summon some kind of authority, but in all likelihood I felt they'd probably meet a similarly tragic end. I decided to leave them to their random fate and continued on my way. Sometimes, I reflected, you just have to let things be.

Coming close to the city centre I noticed that many of the lamp posts were festooned with placards bearing the faces of politicians. An election was on its way. But unlike election posters in much of the rest of the world, which might feature tub-thumping messages or boastful promises, the Swedish politicians looked mild-mannered and insipid. Most wore glasses and oozed the word 'sensible' from every pore in their clear-complexioned faces. One imagined that they were posing for the photographer, momentarily pulled away from some family ritual such as putting the children to bed, in order to utter their soundbites – more teachers in schools; 250,000 new jobs; protect our welfare; less immigration; a better Sweden for all. Their sober messages hardly made it look like an election to get excited about.

When I reached the old centre of Lund the streets had quietened, compared to my earlier visit. Most of the shops were now closed but I noticed a supermarket that was still open and went inside. I was looking for a bottle of wine to take back to my motel room but I walked all around the supermarket searching without success. I asked a girl stacking shelves where the wine was and she led me to an aisle and pointed to some half-dozen bottles on the lowest shelf. I bent down an picked one up, noticing that it had some dust on it. On the label it said *alkoholfri*. I put it down again and resumed my search.

But it proved fruitless. I was dimly aware that alcohol had been prohibited in Sweden in the past and that alcohol-starved Swedes used to pour off the ferries arriving in Denmark with empty shopping trolleys, staggering back on with them full. For years, Copenhagen slang for 'a drunk' was 'a Swede', but I couldn't believe that the alcohol prohibition was still in force. After all, I had been in Swedish bars on several occasions in the past and I hadn't noticed anything amiss.

I decided to ask someone for help. A shopper with a basket filled with salads and meats looked to be an archetypal young Swede. His healthy countenance, tailored tight-fitting suit and immaculately coiffured straw blond hairdo marked him out as someone who would likely speak better English than most English people. I asked him if I was going loopy because I had circled the store several times without being able to find any booze apart from some bottles of reduced alcohol lager. No, he told me, I was not going mad. Had I not heard that you need a special license to buy alcohol for home consumption? There was a single shop, he said, where you could go and buy alcohol and what's more it was nearby. But it was closed, he said. It was always closed in the evenings. I asked why. Because that is when people most want alcohol, he explained patiently, so that is why it was closed. But I could go there in the morning, he added.

Beaten, I bought some dried sausage meat and rye bread for my dinner and left the supermarket. I wandered through narrow cobbled streets to the medieval heart of the town where the university and the cathedral were located. Students sat outside pizza restaurants beneath outdoor heaters and I passed a few bars full of young people. At one, a modern cafe/bistro affair inserted into a half-timbered building, I stopped and was momentarily tempted to go inside. The clientele all seemed to be students – this was a university town after all – and they were dressed impeccably with a studied casualness. I looked closer and saw that hardly anyone seemed to be drinking any alcohol. Instead, in front of most of the patrons stood a fruit juice, a frothy coffee or a glass of water, with only the occasional glass of wine or bottle of craft beer on display.

I looked at their radiant faces, their white teeth and noted their *légèreté de l'être*, and I couldn't help but contrast the scene with my own university days two decades ago, where my cohort would likely have been wearing donkey jackets, eating chips with curry sauce and drinking subsidised lager in the student union bar. Back then we lived in often filthy rented houses, we never seemed to have any money, and half of the conversations revolved around how to overthrow Margaret Thatcher's government. What strange historical force was afoot here? Didn't they know their futures were being plundered while they sat there drinking their mocktails? Why weren't they angry?

The evening was clear but cold. You could almost feel the last ebb of summer's heat as it faded away. Blinds were pulled down over ancient leaded windows and rooks cawed loudly from some nearby trees. I walked to the park beside the almost thousand year-old cathedral, noticing the door was open. Stepping inside I entered into another existential zone. Its capacious inner space was lit by candles and a residual feeling of centuries of worship, dusty sacraments and ancient power suffused the space.

Only a couple of other people were present, sitting in quiet contemplation on the pews, and I walked slowly down the central aisle towards the high altar. Above it a *trompe l'oeil* of a haloed Jesus glowed with a golden light. I allowed the feeling of the numinous to seep into me as I moved slowly past arches carved from immense sandstone blocks. A flight of stone steps led down into the crypt. I had been here once before, a decade ago, but the crypt had been closed at the time. This time it appeared to be open and a welcoming light spilled out from the room below, beckoning me down. I descended.

The softly lit chamber housed several stone sarcophagi. I gazed at them, sensing an inert presence that whispered of forgotten stories and decayed authority. Inside lay the white bones of bishops and it felt as if a deathly chill had seeped out from under the stone lids, gathering in the corners of the room. Aesthetically the graves were all different, displaying mixed styles of decoration, with some more elaborate than others. The vaulted ceiling above was supported by numerous pillars, one of which was carved into the shape of a man.

A plaque explained that legend says this pillar was the petrified remains of Jätten Finn, a troll who had helped to build the cathedral in return for the heart and eyes of the builder Esbern Snare. If Esbern could not guess the troll's name before the building was complete, went the story, he would forfeit his organs of sight and feeling. Luckily for him he heard a female troll sing out Jätten Finn's name while he was lying beside a nearby river. He returned to the almost finished cathedral and called out the name of the troll. Finn became so angry that he tried to pull down the whole building by ripping out the pillars in the crypt, but instead he was turned to stone and has remained stuck there ever since.

I wandered around the crypt for a few minutes looking at the inscriptions and trying to parse the contrast between the modern world outside and the ancient world of death and myth entombed within. I remembered reading that beneath the stone flags on the floor were also said to lie the remains of the Celtic magical warrior Fionn mac Cumhaill. Could this be true? I stooped down and touched the cold floor with my fingers, hoping to feel an answer. This mix of magic and religion, legend and history beguiled me. For the Church, when it was erecting its great cathedrals in Europe, had favoured places bordering wilderness. These hinterlands, populated by heathens (literally, people living in small houses on heathland), and pagans (literally, people living in the country) provided areas rich in souls for conversion.

Scandinavia came late to Christianity, only turning its back on the old gods under decree from the Viking leader Harald Bluetooth. The Jelling Stones in Denmark's Jutland peninsula still bear the inscribed runes which read "*King Harald bade these memorials to be made after Gorm, his father, and Thyra, his mother. The Harald who won the whole of Denmark and Norway and turned the Danes to Christianity.*"

Lund Cathedral was founded not long after the Jelling Stones were inscribed. For the bishops who held their seats of power here, it was a fortress from which to spread the word of God. And the word of this new god, as interpreted by a heretic who died on a cross, was their weapon. For the first time, in these parts, religion became something that was taught by middlemen from a pulpit, rather than experienced directly in the open-air cathedral of nature.

And now, the funny thing is, almost a millennium later, Harald's legacy as a uniter of peoples under the banner of Christianity has been co-opted as a wireless short wave radio technology standard, managed by the US-based Bluetooth Special Interest Group which, fittingly, has one of its offices in Malmö. The symbol that appears at the top of screens on mobile devices indicating a Bluetooth connection is a blind rune that merges the Viking king's initials H (Harald) and B (Blåtand).

Whether the assertion that the fractious pagan tribes of Scandinavia were united by Christianity or not is open to some debate, but the fact that Bluetooth's name is now a byword for digital connectedness in our modern age is faintly ironic when one considers that history adjudged Harald as a weakling, known for running away in battle, heaping up defeats and caving in to Christian zeal. And how fitting that technology and progress should be the new religions of our age, with hand-held gadgets replacing rosary beads and Steve Jobs standing in for Jesus.

Ascending the steps once more I noticed that the two other people had left and that I was all alone in the cathedral. I made for the door, keen to get back into the world of the living. Outside, a small commotion attracted my attention. The sound of voices raised in merriment was mingled with the sharp caw of birds on what should have been a quiet Monday evening. I wandered over to the crowd making the human noises and saw several dozen black-robed students standing on a terrace drinking champagne from tall fluted glasses. Clearly some kind of graduation event was occurring.

The university was one of the oldest seats of learning in the world, having been founded as a medieval university by Franciscan monks in 1425 to accompany the cathedral next door. The building the graduates were stood before was a palatial – if somewhat busy – affair, a farrago of classical antiquity featuring columns of parthenaic grandeur, topped by four sphinxes which looked down on the formal gardens. A cherub trumpeted water skywards from an ornate fountain, adding a touch of Elysian garnish to the scene.

But whatever noise the graduates were making at their ball, it was drowned out by the raucous calls of hundreds of rooks in a nearby oak tree. I wandered over to it to take a closer look. It was a large tree, probably planted around the time the modern university's main building was being raised in the latter half of the nineteenth century. Around it plastic DayGlo barriers had been erected to form an exclusion zone. A sign warned passers-by to beware of falling branches, but that didn't seem to be the whole story.

Rooks, I knew from observation in Cornwall, form large flocks at the end of summer and set up rookeries in mature trees. I glanced over at an adjacent grass lawn and saw it to be covered in dark feathers. Bending down, I saw that they were indeed black feathers, all cut at sharp angles. What's more, a metal dumpster parked under a nearby tree was overflowing with these sharply-scissored black feathers. I smelled a massacre. I had no idea what had happened but it looked as if thousands of these intelligent but bothersome birds had been hoovered out of their nests and put through a wood chipper. I shuddered at the thought of it, deciding to leave the scene and head back to my motel.

It took the best part of an hour to walk back. The pair of chickens had gone, and there was no sign of carnage on the road. Perhaps they had managed to cross it (why?) and had made it to safety somewhere. I walked over the immense parking lot of the shopping mall adjacent to my hotel. Long black looping skid marks on the asphalt indicated boy racers. My mind conjured up night-time hot-rodders in souped-up Volvos blaring Swedish rap music and throwing Max Burger cups out of the windows. Probably. I walked into the motel. The same woman I had met earlier on was there. She said she was on the late shift. "Is there a bar here?" I asked. Of course, she replied, telling me to take a seat at the reception. I did so and she appeared a moment later with a bottle of Absolut vodka. "Small or large?"

I drank the vodka and felt the pleasant sensation of the day's travails drifting away. What a strange place I am in, I thought to myself. I was perched on a high chair at the reception of a hotel that was like the bastard child of an IKEA store and a shipping container, drinking vodka under a spotlight and listening to muzak being piped through speakers hidden behind a tropical plant. The woman was apologetic for my earlier experience with the taxi driver. I told her not to worry about it, that every country has its cheats, but she seemed to want to make a wider point. I asked her about the upcoming elections and she said that things were going awry in her country, that the path would have to change or else bad things would happen. "I am voting for one of the smaller parties", she said when I asked.

I had another vodka and then one more as I chatted with the receptionist. The shift changed and the chatty woman was replaced by a sleepy-looking man with dark rings under his eyes. I went to sit in the breakfast bar to read one of the free newspapers deposited there. Mostly it was filled with the same news as the English-language newspapers – insurgent Jihadis, updates on the lives of celebrities, and the purported Russian menace. There were pictures of a flood somewhere in Sweden, and images of distraught householders standing up to their knees in water inside their homes. I folded the newspaper, drained my glass and got up to leave. I thought that maybe the vodka was on the house, given how informally it had been given out, but the man with the tired face handed me a bill and asked for my credit card.

Locating my room up on the second floor I pushed the plastic key into its slot and the door opened electronically. I went inside and sat on the bed. Physically I was tired from the day's exertions, but my mind was feverishly alive from the vodka on an empty stomach. I turned on the television and flicked through the channels, eventually settling on a documentary about the American actress Lauren Bacall, who had died a week before. The talking heads on screen reminisced about her greatness and ability as an actress, how she had taken Hollywood by storm, and about her stormy marriage with Humphrey Bogart. It was a whole life summed up in an hour of plaudits.

I turned off the screen with the remote and sat looking unfocusedly around the dimly lit room. It seemed reasonable to think right then that great achievements were the domain of mysterious Others whose Chthonic powers elevated them to the top of humanity's ant heap. These chosen few were permitted to make their deposit on the great pile of Culture, and when they died BBC producers could make earnest biopics about them, to be syndicated to Swedish public broadcasters and relayed to concrete motels in retail hinterlands. But did such things happen by chance or by the application of will? How might one break out of the monotony and the conformity and achieve... something? And if something is achieved, then what lasting value would it hold? What even was the point of trying? Like everyone, I assumed, I wanted my life to add up to at least something. Something, they say, is better than nothing at all.

I caught my reflection in the mirror on the wall at the end

of the bed. I looked shifty. Bedraggled, weighted down, drowning almost. Perhaps that's why I usually avoided looking in mirrors, for fear of seeing the shape-shifter that liked to play out a rhythm with my life, pulling me down into its black realm and then releasing me as it saw fit, allowing me to rise into the sharp light and gulp in great breaths of air. That is what life had become, I felt, an endless journey from one realm to the other. Sighing, I got out Marcus Aurelius and began to read. What could a privileged Roman emperor possibly say that would have value so far into the future, I wondered. I read a few pages and stumbled across this passage.

Remember how long you have been putting this off, how many times you been given a period of grace by the gods and not used it. It is high time now for you to understand that the universe of which you are a part, and the governor of that universe of whom you constitute an emanation: and that there is a limit circumscribed to your time – if you do not use it to clear away your clouds, it will be gone, and you will be gone, and the opportunity will not return.

The words flew across the aeons, and they rang absolutely true. How many of us have put off doing something that we know is right *deep down* because we found life getting in the way and chose instead to procrastinate? I thought of the dead bishops in the crypt earlier on, of how great their power and fame must have seemed back in their day, and how now the only thing to remind us of their existence were some cold slabs of stone with Latin inscriptions. Had they left the world a better or a worse place?

I put down the book and turned off the light. As I fell asleep I had a tingling feeling of certainty that I was going somewhere I had never before dared to go.

Chapter 8. Lost in Translation

"A man who speaks three languages is called trilingual. A man who speaks two languages is called bilingual. A man who speaks one language is called an Englishman."

– Spanish witticism

The trains in Sweden were spacious, clean and well maintained. It was as if they were replaced every few months, perhaps whenever they got dirty. They were painted purple. Each carriage had several flat screen TVs presenting rolling news coverage interspersed with little trivia questions in place of adverts: "Flooding has forced hundreds to abandon their homes... Is a bassoon a percussion, a string or a wind instrument? – find out in a minute...". I sat and looked out of the window as the muddy countryside flashed past. I was damned if I was going to walk the rest of the way to Söderåsen, slogging along tracks and putting up with waterlogged shoes and socks. There would be plenty of time for all that when I was actually *in* the forest.

I had spent the morning and early afternoon wandering around Lund and sheltering from the incessant rain inside the tropical hothouse at the botanic gardens. There I had lounged beneath banana trees and hibiscus plants reading more of Marcus Aurelius's meditations and drinking tea at the visitors' cafe. After this I had treated myself to another Max burger with fries (adding another 3.3kg of carbon to my footprint), for that was more or less the only affordable food on offer to match my constrained budget. It was already late afternoon by the time I got off at Teckomatorp, a brief stop in a small town a few miles north of Lund, and the rain was coming down in torrents again.

I headed to a tiny shelter and waited for the bus whose number I had scrawled on the receipt from my Max burger.

Looking at the timetable inside the shelter I saw that I had just missed the connection and would have to wait an hour for the next bus. Another man hurried in out of the rain and we stood shoulder to shoulder in this narrow shelter. It is said that when travelling in Scandinavia if you initiate casual conversation with another traveller you will have broken a taboo and marked yourself out as a foreign fool. The author Michael Booth tested out this theory for his amusing book *The Almost Nearly Perfect People*, and I had no wish to replicate his experiment with this man.

And so together we stood in uncomfortable silence for an entire hour. I was in such close proximity to the other man that I could hear his breath rise and fall. During this time his mobile phone rang perhaps twenty times, although he didn't answer it on any occasion. The first couple of times he looked at it and issued a gruff curse under his breath. After that he simply ignored its plinkety-plonkety ringtone.

Eventually the tension became too much for me to bear and I offered him a sheepish grin and an inane comment about someone 'really wanting to get through'. The man looked at me in disdain and turned away. I shut up, resolving never again to try and make smalltalk on this journey. If it hadn't been belting down with rain I would have gone and waited somewhere else. I began to feel sick.

Eventually the bus arrived and relieved the tension. I stepped aboard and read out the name of the place I wanted to travel to, as it was written on my receipt. "I want to go to Skäralids", I said to the driver. I was speaking in Danish, although I hoped I had said it in a sufficiently Swedish way. After all, I reasoned, the Scandinavian languages are sufficiently alike that, in theory at least, a Dane can understand a Swede, just as well as she can understand a Norwegian, and vice versa. It's a bit like a Cockney speaking with a Glaswegian. The bus driver, a heavy set man perhaps in his sixties, turned off the engine and looked at me with what seemed to be distaste.

"*Khva*?" he grunted.

"Skäralids", I replied.

"*Khva!*" he said again, squinting at me and popping a cigarette between his lips like a desperado in a spaghetti western. He then stood up and, brushing past me, stepped off the bus and into the shelter. There was the click of a lighter and then a cloud of white smoke. He studied me for a moment before unleashing a stream of invective, jabbing his cigarette at me as he let rip.

I got the gist of what he was saying.

"When will you lot have the decency to actually learn how to speak Swedish?" he burbled. "You can't even pronounce the words right and then you expect us to understand what the hell you're talking about." He glared at me and blew smoke out of his nostrils. There was nobody else on the bus except the man who refused to answer his phone, and he just sat there staring at me and the bus driver with complete indifference. I realised my error.

I tried to respond in my invented Swedish accented Danish but any confidence I'd had in my voice had now drained away. "*Khva, khva*", he repeated, arching his eyebrows in mock incomprehension.

"I'm not Danish", I explained, in English. "I'm from England."

"Eenglish?" he said, eyes bulging at the thought. He considered this for a moment and then returned to his rant, this time switching to Skåneish accented English. "Bollsheet!" he ejaculated. There was no confusing this last word. He continued "No Eenglish speak Daneesh."

I begged to differ and explained how I had lived in Denmark in the past, and apologised for my poor attempt at mimicking Swedish using bad Danish. He considered this for a moment, smiling to himself and shaking his head as if in disbelief that a Danish-speaking Englishman should appear out of nowhere and try to speak Swedish in the hinterlands of Skåne on *his* bus on a rainy Tuesday afternoon. A thought occurred to him. "Manchester United", he said, as if it were a statement.

"Um, yes", I replied. "Actually my father was from Manchester. He was a footballer when he was young. He even played for Manchester City. In their junior team."

"Ceety?".

"Yes", I replied.

It wasn't much to offer but it seemed to satisfy the driver that I wasn't making this up. He stubbed out the cigarette and boarded the bus again, giving me a friendly slap on the back as he did so. "Manchester", he said again smilingly, as though the place brought back warm memories, which I thought unlikely. Settling himself again in his seat and turning on the engine he looked at me and said that sound again. "*Khva, khva.*" It sounded like he had catarrh stuck in his throat that he was trying to expel.

"No *ska* but *khva* … you go *Khva*ralids", he explained.

"*Khva*ralids", I dutifully repeated. "How much?"

I opened my wallet and proffered at 100 kroner note at him. That should cover it, I thought. But the bus driver's eyes bulged once more. "No!" he spluttered. "Not money. Cart. In Sweden only cart now."

"Oh", I said, putting away the money. It seemed a bit strange paying for a short bus ride with a credit card and I was worried I didn't have enough in my account to cover it. But my anxiety was misplaced and the little printer issued me with a ticket. I sat down. "*Khva!*" said the driver sternly, just so I didn't forget. And finally, in the rearview mirror, "Hey, I joke you, okay?"

"Okay", I replied meekly.

The man who wouldn't answer his phone sat and started at me impassively. I began to entertain the thought that he might be a robot.

73

The countryside of southern Sweden passed by outside. Small towns came and went, one more or less indistinguishable from the next. I had come to the perhaps unfair conclusion long ago that settlements smaller than large cities tended to be unprepossessing chunks of suburbia set down in the landscape. At least that is how it seemed here in the flatlands, for I had never ventured into the mountainous landscapes of the north. The streets and parks were always scrupulously clean and there was usually a small supermarket, a church, a bad pizza takeaway and maybe a Thai restaurant owned by a fifty-something man and his Asian wife. The cultivated countryside, too, could be monotonous in its conformity. See one large field of industrially planted wheat or rape seed and you've seen them all.

Southern Sweden in this respect is remarkably similar to Denmark. They share the same characteristics of orderliness – comfortable and salubrious towns inset in a landscape of gently rolling hills or implacable flatness. Perhaps this shouldn't come as a surprise given that the region of Skåne is separated from Denmark by only a narrow strait and the area was indeed part of Denmark until its return to Sweden after the Battle of Helsingborg in 1710. Neolithic ruins, Viking settlements and stone circles fringe the coastlines, but I doubted I was going to see any on this trip.

I followed our route on the map I had been given. The bus journey only took about half an hour and soon it wasn't cultivated fields we were passing through but scattered stands of woodland. The trees became ever denser and soon enough there were trees on both sides of the road. We passed through a small town and, not long after, the bus suddenly stopped and the door opened. It was time for me to get off. "Remember, *khva!*", the driver shouted to me as I stepped down onto the sodden grass at the side of the road.

The bus drove off and I was left standing beside a dead-straight road that cut through forest as far as I could see in each direction. Heavy, ragged clouds lumbered across the sky above and I knew that another deluge was on the way. I was standing opposite the visitor car park for the national park, although there were only about a half dozen cars parked in it and nobody seemed to be around. My map had an icon of a tent on it at this place, so I walked towards a reddish building set back from the road which seemed the likely camping place. It wasn't, but a couple with back-packs and waterproof maps pointed me in the right direction.

The camping area, when I found it, was set in a natural rock amphitheatre a couple of hundred yards back from the road. There was immaculate green grass, a small wooden building and about five or six large motorhomes. Inside these I could make out faces behind the windows. A note on the door of the wooden building said the reception was situated in a yellow house over the road and was open only in the mornings.

I walked around the campsite looking for a place to pitch my tent. The ground was waterlogged in places from the heavy rains and I eventually picked a spot next to a hedge that was a few inches higher than elsewhere and therefore not as wet. It took only a couple of minutes to get the flimsy little tent up and I immediately began to worry whether it would be able to withstand a serious downpour. I didn't have long to ponder the tent's waterproof capabil-ities as the heavens soon opened up again and I dived in-side and lay on my back listening to the intense rush of rain hitting the single-layered nylon shell just inches above my face. After a while it eased off again and, apart from a few drips, I was happy that it had kept me dry.

But something wasn't quite right. My stomach had been churning ever since I had been waiting for the bus, and now I felt positively ill. The burger I had eaten earlier seemed to be the culprit and I fumbled to unzip the tent as saliva filled my mouth. I jumped out and stood there, bending forwards with my hands on my knees. My breathing was shallow and all I could focus on was the green grass that I felt I was about to throw up on. After a few moments the rush of saliva stopped and I began to feel better.

I straightened up and looked around, noticing the people in the motor homes staring back at me. And then I was suddenly violently sick. When the water cleared from my eyes I looked up, embarrassed. The motor homers stared back at me from within their comfortable metal boxes with a 'what's he going to do next' looks on their faces. Great, I thought to myself. This was my opening act in this amphitheatre. There's nothing like making a good impression on arrival.

Following this performance I was too ashamed to hang around any longer so I zipped up the tent and went out to explore my new surroundings. It was early evening and the dirty-looking clouds continued to drift close overhead, threatening yet more rain. Would this weather ever let up? I had my doubts, so I put on my waterproof poncho and headed out of the camp site in the direction of the forest. The trees, crowned with mist, loomed up before me on the other side of the empty highway.

I followed a path over a busy little stream and soon found myself walking across a green expanse towards a lake. Mowed grass clippings plastered my shoes as I squelched across the field. The lake was placid under the heavy sky and on its glassy surface a family of white swans glided. I stood and watched for a few minutes as they cut through the water with serene indifference to the honking ducks that were splashing around nearby. Heavy bodied mosquitoes hung clumsily above the surface of the water and floated around my head, and a sweet freshness filled the air, revitalising me.

By now the thickening clouds had reduced the light level and it was beginning to get dark. The forest, whose threshold I was now stood upon, exuded a damp earthy smell that was both inviting and slightly ominous. I felt a strong urge to venture at least a short distance into its dark interior before night fell and so I crossed a bridge over a corner of the lake and took a path that led into it. The steep path was worn and wet and my shoes slipped on the almost frictionless mud as I scrambled up it. Within moments I was enclosed in semi-darkness, with any feeble light there was being blocked out by the closed canopy above me. And the trees! They were huge beeches, thick and straight and with giant gnarled roots that crawled across the path like knotty arthritic limbs. I paused and savoured the atmosphere of this place. It was as if I had crossed a subtle threshold and entered a space somewhat apart from human terms.

As my eyes adjusted to the light I could make out puffy white objects poking out of the forest floor. Mushrooms, lots of them. They were not the smallish mushrooms I was used to seeing in England, but huge bulbous ones with white caps. I bent down and looked at the closest cluster and was surprised to see that they were being devoured in slow motion. The creatures doing the devouring were huge black slugs, as big as Mars bars and with bodies like shiny liquorice. Looking around I saw all sorts of other mushrooms and fungus too. Some were flat and brown like parasols, others grew in yellow clusters and still more were bold and red like huge boiled sweets.

Some of the trees were studded with large solid-looking fungal growths, and I noticed that these trees were either dead or dying, and perhaps this fungus was doing the killing, or at least helping along the act of dying. Beyond the margins of the forest a white miasma was creeping up from the lake and the shrill cry of waterfowl seemed to indicate that night would soon fall. I decided to head back to the campsite and have an early night.

Returning along the slippery path I once again emerged into the civilised space of the grassy park, the ornamental lake, the visitor centre restaurant and car park. Next to the lake stood the handsome ochre building I had seen earlier.

It was built in the local vernacular country style with a low roof and barn red walls. It appeared to be a restaurant, although no people were around to animate it. My mind became filled with images of little plates covered with rye bread and pickled herrings, devilled eggs sprinkled with red caviar, smoked salmon and cold meat platters. I felt hungry and my stomach began to rumble in sympathy with my mind. Crossing the road on the way back to the campsite I paused to allow a truck to pass. It was loaded with lumber and lit up like a Christmas tree. It roared past me and I watched as it receded to a bright distant speck on the long highway.

Although I had given most of my food to the beggar in Lund I still had a few staples, such as a bag of rice and stock cubes, but had nothing to cook with. My admittedly short-sighted plan had been to heat up food on an open fire of hedgerow wood as I exercised my right of *allemansrätt*. But reality had proved somewhat different to the fantasy and I now found myself on a soggy patch of grass bearing a notice board with a long list of 'Do Not' regulations stipulated on it, one of which was lighting fires. In any case, I doubted I could find anything dry enough to burn. I had noticed that the wooden building at the campsite contained a communal kitchen, but at this hour it was of no use to me as it was on the other side of a security coded door that was locked.

I began to look around at the trees and bushes. I was in luck. A hazel was weighed down with heavy ripe nuts and I pulled them off in pairs, filling my pockets. Not far from that was an apple tree, and although the fruit were quite small and hard a test bite revealed they were surprisingly sweet. The only other thing I could find worth eating was a handful of dandelion leaves. I took my haul and climbed up a rocky escarpment that rose up above the campsite. Perched on a small cliff I found a fist-sized rock which I used to crack open the nuts, which I then wrapped in the dandelion leaves. This dandelion nut sandwich was washed down with swigs from my water bottle. The apples provided a dessert.

As I savoured my meagre meal I looked down at the scene below me. My puny tent appeared to be little more than a fungal oddity that had popped up in the grass beside the motorhomes, one of which, I noted, even had a small car hitched to its rear. Warm light oozed from their windows and I could make out a family eating their evening meal at a table as the flicker of a television cast blue light outwards.

I felt a pang of homesickness for my own family and wondered, not for the last time, what a soggy Englishman with a gash on his leg was doing alone in a tiny tent on the edge of a forest in Sweden. If I chose, I reasoned, I could pack up in the morning, get back on that bus and be in Copenhagen the same evening. It would make for a dull two weeks but at least I would be warm and looked after and perhaps I *would* go around the businesses in the city and try to drum up some business as my wife wanted me to. These were the thoughts I had as I finished the last apple and swept the broken nut shells off the boulder I had been using as an anvil.

As I was making my way back down to the campsite, hopping from one rock to another, the first big drop of rain fell on me. Great lumps of dark clouds with fuzzy undersides shambled across the sky towards me and the fading edges of the forest disappeared in a blur of rain. The downpour hit suddenly. I ran to the tent and unzipped it. Once inside I turned on the small headlight and put on the thick woollen jumper that had been taking up so much room in my pack. Summer was at an end and I was familiar enough with these latitudes to know that even in late August it could get downright cold at night.

I then wriggled inside my sleeping bag and lay back on the thin air mattress. For a while I listened to the sound of the rain, which was now more of a roar that a patter, and felt a deep satisfaction to be lying so close to the Earth. It had been a long time since I had last done this. I tried to fall asleep but the elemental roar of the water kept me from doing so. I turned on the light, got out the copy of *Soulcraft* and began to read.

Many again are beginning to hear the soul's call and want to follow it into the unknown. But there are fears. What will happen to me? What will others think? There are very few societal practices or values to support us on the journey. When the soul is heard but not engaged, we fall into a type of sorrow, a soul depression.

I lowered the pages. It was uncanny, the way both of the books I had brought with me seemed to be echoing everything that I was thinking and feeling. I was aware that we had come to a pass in our human condition. That to find answers we would have to descend into a deep and dark place, and that this would likely not be a pleasant experience. I read on:

The descent – and the darkness into which it leads – have their own value; the journey to soul is not a misfortune or a necessary evil. In Western cultures, we rarely enter the underworld except when abducted, like Eurydice or Persephone, by a great loss or depression. Then the descent can be harrowing indeed as we enter a blackness of fear we won't escape. With no guides or allies, no preparation or relevant skills, and few inner resources to call upon, we're not likely to enjoy the journey. But we may yet benefit from the experience. Better to be carried off than not go at all. Abduction is the soul's way of pulling us down towards it if we will not voluntarily step through the gates and over the edge.

I read Bill Plotkin's words until my eyes grew tired and then switched off the light and lay back. My nose was just inches from the thin shell of the tent above. It was difficult to put my finger on but it felt as if I was on the edge of something and that a path had mysteriously opened up before me and brought me to this place. The sensation was that I was being guided somewhere, rather than going there of my own volition. I didn't know where I was going or what would happen and, just as Bill Plotkin had written, I was followed by my fears. *What will others think?* I tried to empty my mind and watch these fears pass before me. Viewed with cold neutrality they appeared as rather flimsy and ephemeral, and so I chose to accept them as they were and not let them hinder me. But the question remained... if I ignored my fears, was I ready then to receive whatever would come next? Is one ever ready for such things?

Chapter 9. Rain

"The world is full of magic things, patiently waiting for our senses to grow sharper."

– W B Yeats

I awoke in the middle of the night. Outside the rain was still hammering down on the thin shell of the tent and I had the eerie feeling that I was floating. My feet felt wet and the mattress had become hard and cold. It occurred to me that it had deflated and that I was now lying in a deepening puddle. I fumbled for the headlight and, when I turned it on, I saw something flashing inside the tent. The beam of light had caught several drips forming on the ceiling and falling down onto the sleeping bag, which was now glistening and wet.

I cursed and began the process of stuffing anything that mattered into a plastic bag for protection. I had brought a small tea towel with me for drying dishes, and with this I began to mop up the puddle, wringing it out through the flap at the entrance to the tent. I did this for some time but it proved futile as long as the rain continued because the drips were getting bigger and they seemed to be falling more rapidly. And so, with anything of value secured within the plastic bag, I turned out the light and attempted to go back to sleep.

As if that were possible.

The rest of the night became a series of short snatches of slumber punctuated by mopping up sessions with the tea towel. My sleeping bag and clothes continued to soak up the water that was coming through and at some point before dawn, in a state of fatigue, I simply gave in and lay in the blackness as water dripped onto my sodden sleeping bag and my exposed face.

By the time the grey light of dawn had crept over the horizon the rain had eased off a little and I peered out of the tent. During the night it felt as if I was being washed away inside the tent, but no, thankfully I was still in the same place on the slightly raised ground beside the hedge. But the rest of the campsite was several inches deep in water and seemed to have turned into a paddy field. The only positive thing that could be said about this was that the rain had washed away the remains of the Max burger.

I pulled myself out of the tent and opened up the front, inspecting the damage. Everything was wet apart from the few items, including my books, that I had stuffed into the plastic bag. Looking at the grey skies it seemed that the heavens would soon open up again, so there was no point hanging up my sleeping bag and clothes to drip dry. The season suggested autumn and a chilly breeze made the leaves dance in the silver birches near the wooden cabin. Most of the motor homes still had their curtains closed and I imagined how dry and warm and snug it must be inside them. I looked at my meagre supply of food and wondered what I would eat. Perhaps I would be able to get inside the wooden hut, I thought, and so wandered over. The door was still locked but luckily, just at that moment, a woman appeared from within with a towel on her head as if she had just stepped out of the shower. "You are the one in that tent?" she asked with a nod in the direction of the forlorn blue scrap of fabric sitting in its own reflection.

"Sure am", I said sheepishly.

"You are brave sleeping in that!"

"Either brave or stupid", I replied.

She laughed and held the door open for me. "You had better go inside and get dry."

I thanked her and asked what the code for the door was. She gave me the code and told me there was some coffee in the pot inside the hut and that I was welcome to have it. She then picked her way along the path through the flooded site to her motor home. Inside the hut it was warm and dry. Looking not unlike something from a home furnishings catalogue, the hut had a lounge area with tables and chairs, a small kitchen, showers, toilets and a sauna. I poured myself some coffee, hot and black, and added some sugar before sitting down in one of the comfortable chairs. After a few minutes I began to warm up.

The night had been so awful that I had spent most of my waking time thinking about whether or not to throw in the towel and head back to Copenhagen. By about four o'clock in the morning I had made up my mind that this was exactly what I was going to do. If I didn't, I reasoned, I'd probably catch pneumonia and end up with trench foot. My resolve was set: this whole trip had been a stupid idea right from the start and I should have planned it better. What a fool I had been to think I could just walk out without so much as a plan and with hardly any money and expect that it would be okay! Perhaps, I considered, this was the stirrings of a mid-life crisis. Or maybe even some sort of mental illness. I imagined white-uniformed nurses tending to me and an electronic bracelet strapped around my ankle.

But now, sitting in the quiet and the warmth and with a hot cup of coffee in front of me donated by the kind stranger, my resolve to throw in the towel began to appear less appealing than it had done during the night. *Just give it another day*, a voice seemed to whisper. And then something both remarkable and unremarkable happened. As if in symphony with this inner voice a gap opened up in the clouds and the campsite was bathed in soft yellow sunlight. It shone through the windows of the hut and illuminated everything with its buttery brilliance. It refracted and reflected through the leaves of the birch trees creating a dancing pattern of green and white light on every surface in the hut, including my own skin. I smiled to myself. Such a serendipitous sign must be a good thing, a bit of gentle encouragement. I drank the coffee and bathed in the warm glow, looking at nothing but the illuminated leaf shadows dancing in the sunlight on the wall above the fire extinguisher.

A short while later, and after a second cup of coffee, I walked over the road to find the yellow house where the reception was located. I rang on the doorbell and a white-whiskered man answered the door and welcomed me in. With his Benny beard, his measured manner and his neat house, the campsite owner looked like the archetypal Scandinavian male retiree. His house was situated within a well-maintained garden and, there on the driveway, sat a shiny new Volvo. He probably made wooden toys in his spare time and smoked a pipe on special occasions. I told him I'd like to stay for a few nights before heading into the forest and he apologised about the weather and said I could stay there at a lower rate. "The season's over", he said, "and you've just a little tent."

I asked him if I could pitch the tent on a spot by the children's playground that was covered by a roof. "Of course", said the man, who was called Björn. "Did I need to buy food?" He told me I'd need to get the bus to a town further up the highway, saying there was one bus an hour and warning me that they didn't take cash any more 'like everywhere else'.

Even though my clothes were still soggy and wet from my night under nylon I decided to head to the shops immediately. I wandered over to the stop where the bus driver had let me out the previous day. Another huge downpour hit as I waited, although I had my poncho on to prevent me from getting any wetter. After it had passed I looked over at the forest, which seemed to be giving off a mist again, like a rainforest. The bus arrived and I boarded. The town in question, Ljungbyhed, was only about ten minutes away and I figured I could walk it in future if I needed to return. In the tiny supermarket I bought some food and coffee and waited for the bus to return and take me back again.

Ljungbyhed was something of a one-horse town without the horse. Apart from the small supermarket there was a tired-looking shop selling tired-looking electrical equipment, and the standard issue pizzeria. Two teenage boys wearing low-hanging jeans and back-to-front baseball caps sat outside it and half-heartedly chucked snickering volleys at me as I waited for the bus. I ignored them, and soon enough they were distracted by another similarly-clad youth riding past on a noisily buzzing moped. The moped rider slowed outside the pizzeria and held up his middle finger to the teenagers before accelerating away. This caused them some alarm and the two boys immediately forgot about the foreigner wearing a big green poncho standing at a bus stop with shopping bags. They jumped up and disappeared from the scene, leaving their half-eaten pizza in its cardboard box on the table. A couple of sparrows descended and made off with a few crumbs, providing an endnote to what was probably the most dramatic happening in Ljungbyhed that day.

Back at the campsite I moved the tent to the patch of sand beneath the wooden roof in the children's play area. The school holidays had now passed and I hadn't seen any young kids around the site. I had to move two large black slugs and several dog turds, but once the tent was in place I had my own miniature outbuilding, complete with a picnic table and bench. I managed this just in time, as another cloudburst drenched the landscape and caused the flooding on the site to rise another couple of inches so that even my former camping spot was now underwater. I then went back inside the hut and prepared myself a brunch of baguette, with cheese, tomatoes and mayonnaise. Afterwards I sat barefoot at the table while my socks dried on the windowsill and I wrote in my diary.

Trip to local town to buy groceries. A bit of a depressing place with two teenage boys outside the pizzeria making fun. What is it with these Swedish teenagers? Mind you, it probably wouldn't be any different in England. Another thing - I can't seem to be able to pronounce Swedish place names as no bus driver has yet understood me.

I trailed off... I couldn't think of much to write about, so I got out *Soulcraft* and entered Bill Plotkin's surreal world of soul encounters, vision quests, talking trees and the descent into darkness. Modern civilisation, I read, was in a state of juvenility, unable to 'grow up'. Furthermore, established religion tends to only concern itself with the nebulous 'spirit', ignoring or suppressing the individual soul which each of us possesses. He quotes some native American wisdom which says there are two dances in life: the dance of survival (holding down a job, earning money, buying food, etc.) and the sacred dance, which entails delving down within ourselves to discover what we are made of.

I read for a couple of hours and then, after some lunch, took a nap inside the tent. When I awoke the rain had stopped and the sun was shining. Water vapour rose like spirits from the rocks around the campsite and the whole scene shimmied as if it were rejoicing at the return of the sun. I hung up my sleeping bag on the children's swings and enjoyed the satisfying sight of watching it emit steamy little wisps as it dried.

Later on I went to sit by the lake and watched the resident family of swans as they moved around on the still surface with their serene grace. Down where the lake drained into a small tumbling stream I stood on the wooden bridge and spotted a couple of hawfinches hopping around on the rocks looking for insects. As the sun went down bats and swallows appeared and the sky darkened with thunder-clouds once more. The earlier sun had been only a brief reprieve and I walked quickly back to the tent just as the rain began to fall again. My sleeping bag was still damp but at least on this night, sheltered by the wooden roof, it would not get any wetter.

All in all it had turned out to be a good day. I hadn't really done anything in particular other than adjust to my surroundings and further contemplate the wisdom of the two minds I carried in my backpack. It was as if I were getting ready for my journey, clearing the decks and waiting in an airlock. I wanted all of my senses intact and in tune to perceive the nature of the reality away from the human-centred world – and it felt exciting to anticipate. I went to bed early, contemplating a passage I had read earlier in Marcus Aurelius's *Meditations*:

If you set yourself to your present task along the path of true reason, with all determination, vigour, and good will: if you admit no distraction, but keep your own divinity pure and standing strong, as if you had to surrender it right now; if you grapple this to you, expecting nothing, shirking nothing, but self-content with each present action taken in accordance with nature and a heroic truthfulness in all that you say and mean – then you will lead a good life. And nobody is able to stop you.

Chapter 10. Whispers from the past

"Life can only be understood backwards, but it must be lived forwards."

– Søren Kierkegaard

The next day the rain was so heavy that I didn't emerge from the cabin until it had begun to ease off in the late afternoon. I spent the day reading, drinking coffee and gazing out of the windows at the sodden ground and the slate grey sky. I read some tourist leaflets about the local area and, noticing some Viking runes on one of them, on a whim I carved them into my rowan staff with the Swiss army knife. I had no idea what the runes meant but the effect was pleasing.

I hoped the rain would wash itself out at some point and I wasn't disappointed. By the time I emerged from the hut and got out on the trail it was early evening. The ground beneath my feet was spongy and soft as I passed beneath the stately beeches and ventured out into one of the northern sections of the forest. I was walking swiftly, conscious of the limited light remaining and not pausing much to look around. The brisk exercise felt good after being cramped up all day and I proceeded along one of the higher trails that skirted the cliffs above the gorge. It passed through an area that was littered with the remains of long-abandoned crofts. These mostly took the form of piles of boulders, moss-covered and half-buried by leaf litter. Some were enclosed by stone walls that were slowly sinking back into the forest floor. I stood in the centre of one of these enclosures and tried to imagine the farmers toiling to move the boulders into place for the walls and the houses. In the eerie quiet of the early evening there was a sense of great time passing and of things lost and forgotten.

The land that was now a forest had been extensively managed and farmed since the bronze age, around four thousand years ago. When the glaciers of the last ice age retreated, broad-leaved temperate species of tree colonised the fresh topsoils that had formed atop the newly exposed rock. Hunter-gathering tribes from the south and east had migrated northwards as the forests re-established and became filled with wild game, including reindeer. Birch and Scots pine gave way to hazel and black alder as the climate warmed, and the cold-loving reindeer retreated further north to be replaced by bears, wolves, bison and elk.

It was only relatively recently – nine to six thousand years ago – that the ecosystem had matured to the state where oak, wych elm, lime and ash had found their ecological niches, making the forest too dense for the larger animals, such as bison and wild ox. Humans likely gave them a helping push towards local extinction, and these species were replaced by the more familiar animals we know today: red deer, fox and wild boar.

So by the time the Neolithic farmers appeared on the scene the forest ecosystem was rich in life and ripe for exploitation. They practiced a form of slash and burn agriculture, ring-barking trees and allowing them to wither and die before setting the area ablaze. These fires temporarily enriched the soils with potash and the dead roots of the trees continued to rot below ground, fertilising it enough for the farmers to plant grain. This fertility boost would likely have lasted a few short years before the soils were exhausted and the swidden farmers, who were highly mobile, moved onto the next area for cultivation.

In their wake the cleared areas started out again on the long road to ecological climax, with colonising species of grass and other ground cover plants appearing first. These were grazed by the goats, sheep and pigs the farmers kept, attracting other grazing animals which were hunted for their meat. Thorny and tough species of plant survived, creating protective areas for other saplings to spring up, and it would not have been too long before the area was covered in secondary forest and the canopy once more closed above.

Over the following millennia this area of forest was slowly settled by a growing population of humans and from about 200 CE until the end of the 19th century the forest was farmed as a network of fields and coppiced woodland. Cistercian monks travelling here in 1551 recorded that some two hundred and fifty farms dotted the forest, and by the 17th century vast tracts were taken over and enclosed by the Crown. Large estates formed and these earned their money chiefly from pig farming, with the animals being allowed to roam freely beneath the oaks and beeches as they foraged for nuts and acorns. Wood was also harvested and sold and in general the land was exploited less heavily than it had been by the small scale farmers. A map of the forest survives from 1764, when the area was known as Kvärk, and on it are depicted places with names such as Skällebacken (Skull Hill) and Järnhatten (Iron Helmet). From this map the area appears to have been heavily settled.

Given that the nuts and acorns were now valuable as feed for the Crown's pigs, locals were not permitted to cut down the trees. By this time immense mature oak trees had grown and these were valuable for shipbuilding and fortifications. As such they became the property of the Danish Crown, and later, in the wars of the 17th and 18th century when Denmark fought Sweden for possession of Skåne, Swedish insurgents hid out in the forest and used a network of natural caves and holes in the cliffs to evade the Danish forces. Eventually Sweden won the war but during the fighting the forests were badly damaged.

After the war the forest suffered still more at the hands of the settlers as the population boomed once more. The largest trees were again felled for shipbuilding and construction, others were cut for fuel and the smaller trees went to make fencing. People living on the low-lying plains around the forest needed as much wood as they could get their hands on for cooking and construction and, by the 18th century, the trees of Söderåsen were largely felled and the ground was covered in heather. These heaths were regularly set alight and cleared to allow grazing animals to live on the denuded land, and by 1812, where there had once stood a large and diverse forest, most of the plateau was now open heathland covered in grazing animals. Alarmed by this deterioration the Swedish Crown issued an edict to protect and regenerate the land. Grazing animals were expelled, further enclosure laws were enacted and plantation projects were put into action.

This succeeded in regenerating the tree cover but calamity struck again during the Second World War when many of the trees were felled to make charcoal for woodgas-powered vehicles. After the war the forest was allowed to regenerate once again, and on 13 June 2001 Sweden's King Carl XVI inaugurated Söderåsen as Sweden's newest national park. Throughout its long history of over-exploitation, dieback and revival, the inaccessible slopes and gullies of the gorge, one of the national park's main features, had remained more or less untouched by humans, making it a tiny oasis of ancient continuity in an otherwise tamed and de-wilded landscape.

Scattered around Söderåsen are the graves of the long-departed farmers and their families. The more ancient ones take the form of stone squares and circles, with sunken hollows at the centre indicating long-gone tomb robbers. I stumbled across a few of them as I rambled through the woods, and in one case I came across a huge cairn of rocks that seemed to have a blocked up door in the side of it. I wondered what could be inside but it was getting late and I was a little lost, having strayed from the marked path, so I thought it better to let the mound of stones keep its secrets.

The park's guidebook says there are almost five thousand land clearance cairns dotted around the forest. Archaeologists have found pollen from cultivated grain in this area, allowing them to accurately date the presence of the farmers who built these cairns. From their research it's clear to see that what is now a peaceful forest of giant beech trees was once practically bustling with inhabitants. Even the beech trees are a relatively recent arrival in ecological time, appearing just a few hundred years before the birth of Christ. During the successive clearances of Söderåsen the beeches have repeatedly colonised the exhausted soils, quickly forming an impenetrable canopy and blocking out the light to give themselves hegemonic control over the ecosystem.

Beech forests can be beautiful and calming places, but appearances can be deceptive. In spring and summer the fresh and clean greenery of their leaves is dazzling, and in autumn the warm russet colours are enough to gladden even the most jaded of souls. But the mere fact that they represent such a dominant and seemingly permanent climax species makes for a low level of biodiversity and it can be positively spooky walking around silent beech forests in failing light without the twitter of birdsong or the rustle of a hedgehog in a pile of leaves. All that seemed to remain in Söderåsen as I walked around on that silent evening were the ghosts of the departed farmers and the spirits of the land.

But just as I was thinking these thoughts about how empty the forest seemed, and as if to prove me wrong, a fox suddenly appeared about a hundred paces ahead of me. It paused and looked at me for a moment before swiftly and stealthily moving on. So swift was its movement that it seemed to glide without making a sound as it disappeared between the trees. I chased after it, wondering where it had disappeared to. But it was faster than I was and it had disappeared without a trace. Night was falling fast and I thought I had better get out of the forest before it became too dark to see.

As I turned to go I saw a lone figure tramping through the forest towards me. He was a stumpy man with an unkempt beard and grubby clothes. I nodded a greeting as we passed, hailing him with my staff. But apart from a swift glance my way he didn't acknowledge me and I was left wondering whether he dwelled in the forest like some sort of Radagast the Brown.

Chapter 11. Dust and stones

"If you don't read the newspapers, you're uninformed. If you read the newspapers, you're mis-informed."

– Mark Twain

The next day the rain held off and I spent the entire day walking the forest trails. By late afternoon a golden glow had suffused the trim of the bulbous hanging clouds, scattering sunlight onto the leaves of the trees all around me. Coppery beech leaves, ahead of the season, contrasted sharply against the green leaves which hadn't yet got the memo about autumn coming. I was walking along one of the ridges above the valley and pausing to look out from the visitor viewpoint. Nearby were the remains of some walls built from rocks and a few heaps of stone indicating humans from the past. A small placard in Swedish and English explained what we were looking at.

Stenhagen. The first crofter at Stenhagen – which might be translated as 'Stony Pasture' – was Björn Lagesson, who moved here in 1854 with his wife Catrina Svensdotter and their two year-old daughter Carolina. Five more children arrived in the course of eleven years. Björn died in 1867 and his widow and children stayed on until 1876. After that the place was home to Ola Nilsson and his family for a year before they moved onto the croft known as 'Rallatill'. The next family to live here, parents and five children, lasted from 1877 to 1892. The last crofter in this place was Gottfrid Willy Strahl who moved here with his wife, Marie Sandberg, and three children in 1892. The Strahls stayed for six years and had two more children here, both dead before the age of two. The croft has been empty since the family moved to Västra Sönnarslöv in 1898.

I sat on a wall and looked around at the sad piles of moss-covered rocks spilled across the forest floor. Great trees had thrust up between the stones of the walls, splitting them in half and making a mockery of the efforts of the Lagessons, the Nilssons and the Strahls. I imagined this place as it must have been, with the young families setting out to make their lives here, the horses dragging the heavy rocks from the soil to make way for the plough, the sound of children playing beneath an open sky. I thought of the struggles of widowed Catrina Svensdotter and her six children who soldiered on for nine years after her husband had died. There were dozens of places such as this one in the forest. What a chaotic vortex of change our world is, I thought. Where are the descendants of these people now? Scattered to the four winds, now doubt, working as IT specialists, catering assistants, doctors and dentists.

Once, I myself had bought a piece of land with a jumble of rocks such as these. With the help of some builders I had turned the pile of stones back into a house. I had been living in a beautiful part of southern Spain among the mountains, not too far from the coast. It was an idyllic series of valleys, little touched by the more damaging aspects of the modern world due to the difficult access along the winding mountain roads. The fertile local environment had provided bounteous amounts of fresh food and natural beauty, and a weekly travelling market came by every Thursday meaning that people had little need for supermarkets and big shops.

Our house was built on the side of the highest mountain in the Iberian peninsula and one day I decided to walk up to the top of it. Upon reaching the summit, I saw a terrible sight. On the coast in the distance there stretched an immense sea of white that went all the way to the horizon out to the east. I had heard about the spread of plastic greenhouses that were eating up the land, but from my vantage point I could clearly see it was metastasising the entire region and would soon engulf this place that I had come to cherish as my home. I was alarmed.

Further research revealed that a get-rich-quick mania was sweeping the region and that thousands of illegal wells were being drilled into the underground aquifer to irrigate the greenhouses. The salad crops grown within were exported north to European supermarkets and in their wake they left a trashed landscape of fluttering plastic, depleted aquifers and poisoned wells. Within them, I learned, thousands of African migrants were at work, breathing in the fertilisers and pesticides and living in a state of bonded labour. Furthermore, politicians had decided to divert water from local rivers to irrigate the salad industry, and they now had their sights firmly set on diverting water from our area. If this were allowed to happen it would spell disaster.

The region where I lived was called La Alpujarra and it was famed for its natural beauty and its sense of serenity. When the last Muslim ruler had been expelled from Granada by the Catholic zealots Ferdinand and Isabella it was here that he had brought his people. They settled the valleys and hills, building on the terraces cut into the slopes by the Romans. With their aptitude for managing water and irrigation they turned La Alpujarra into a garden of Eden and there was said to be no terrace or wayside that was not bursting with orange blossom and birdsong. Fields and ridges were overflowing with trees laden with olives, pomegranates, apples and almonds. Mulberry bushes were alive with silkworms, producing a fabric so fine it was in demand as far away as Baghdad. The Moors, as they were known, transformed La Alpujarra into an earthly paradise of flowers, fruit and flowing water, but the real miracle was that it had endured for half a millennium in more or less this state of fecundity, avoiding many of the worst aspects of industrialisation. Until now.

I decided to try and do something to stop this so I set up a local newspaper with the aim of highlighting the threat. I called it the *Olive Press*, and it was run from a small office in the main provincial town of Órgiva. I hadn't the first idea how to produce a newspaper – up until then I'd been an analyst working in the electricity industry – and it took several months of work before the first copy rolled off the printing presses in Granada. Nevertheless when it was eventually up and running it attracted a lot of attention.

Its environmental focus brought in lots of writers who were keen to voice their concern about the ongoing threat to the local area, and every other Thursday, on market day, I was able to sit outside at the local cafe and watch in sheer disbelief as people wandered around with a copy under their arm or, better still, their noses buried in it. It wasn't long before we began to print more copies, spreading them around in nearby towns and villages like pixie dust.

In time it became a great success in every metric apart from one: money. Every month I found that costs seemed to go up, but income remained anaemic at best. Writers and distributors queued up in my office as I handed them envelopes of cash. "Next month we will break even", I told myself and my increasingly concerned wife. For everyone said they enjoyed reading it, but nobody actually wanted to pay for it. Eventually the other editor and I decided to employ a salesman who had been working as an estate agent nearby. The first thing he did was turf out all of the small advertisers who had had trouble keeping up with their payments, and instead shifted his focus onto the bigger fish.

It worked. Soon the money began to roll in and we could relax a little. News of our little half-radical newspaper spread far and wide and we began to expand beyond the borders of our mountain enclave. The print run was ratcheted up to twenty thousand copies every fortnight and we would drive all over the province of Granada delivering them in bundles. Most of the stories we covered focused on local corruption and abuses of the environment and people said things like "We're so glad somebody is saying these things".

But it wasn't long before the complaints started to come in. One estate agent, who was also an advertiser, said he was embarrassed to show a copy of the *Olive Press* to clients visiting Spain. He said it might put them off investing in property in the region. Another businessman cancelled his full-page advert because he said the news within it was 'too realistic'. He wanted to see more happy stories about expats rescuing donkeys and fewer stories about people facing financial ruin from investing in illegal property developments. A bar owner made a point of going around and destroying any copies he found. He said he called it the 'Olive *de*Press'.

The sales manager asked us if we could 'tone it down' and publish some more light-hearted pieces. We resisted and, as a result, money became tight again. Our golden goose sales manager said he would quit and the other editor, who lost no love on me, said I had turned it into a 'tree-hugging hippie rag'. I wrote an editorial about climate change and, on print day, was surprised to see it ending up printed opposite a full page advert for a low-cost airline. I pointed out that this looked like hypocrisy but none of the others in the office saw it as such. They just wanted the money to keep rolling in and had plans to take the paper 'up market'.

A clear split began to emerge between me, the other editor, who was also my business partner, and the sales staff, of which there were now three. People went silent whenever I walked into the office and I would spend days sitting in the same room as the other editor without a word passing between us. And so, eventually, the 'hippie shit' element was surgically removed.

After a year or more of dysfunction I was forced to leave, selling my share to a former *Daily Mail* showbiz columnist, who abandoned its original remit and instead focused on celebrity sightings on the glitzy Costa del Sol. Here there was actual money to be made. The original business went bust with debts, my erstwhile business partner simply disappeared and our names were displayed on a 'wall of shame' by the tax authorities in the city of Granada. Penniless and broken-spirited I had to abandon our Spanish pile of rocks and move back to Copenhagen where we lived for five years in a council flat next to the airport.

I managed four more years working in the news media before quitting, exhausted and disillusioned. Afterwards, when I reflected on this painful lesson, I realised the experience had taught me how money warps and eventually overwhelms anything it comes into contact with. Noble aims, even if they are not strangled at birth, are easy victims once the knives are out. The mainstream media has become a mechanical monster, its only purpose to inflate propaganda for the powerful and egg on the consumption of the planet's remaining resources. It tells us that the news is all about politics and business and celebrities. That we are all in competition with one another and that people are inherently bad. I wanted to play no further part of it for, as Bill Plotkin puts it:

"If we are born to consume then it is a dog-eat-dog world, there is no deeper meaning, no human soul, and creation is just a huge, dumb joke. That's a conclusion you wouldn't want to live with every day; better to distract and deaden yourself with addictions."

Diary entry

I have been reading more of Plotkin and this has got me thinking about initiations. Every culture worth its salt has used initiatory rituals to prepare their young for adulthood – except ours. Many send off their young into wilderness areas where they have to fend for themselves for a period of time.

The Basques traditionally sent theirs out to wander the world for an entire year surviving by their wits and whatever food they could get from strangers. Sometimes, such voyages of discovery would result in the death of the initiate. Does this mean the parents who send off their young on such a daunting journey are bad? Do they not love their offspring like we do?

Of course, it's pointless to try and apply our way of think-ing to these traditional cultural practices. Our own culture would not allow for such things to occur for a whole range of reasons, ranging from health and safety issues to legal suits for abandonment. What's more, our economies would be seriously hampered if too many people became hermits. We have no wise elders left in our societies. Almost. The role of an elder is to provide support to the young who are on the threshold of adulthood and who, more than any-thing, are desperate for guidance as to how to proceed. We got rid of our elders in our rush to modernity; their very existence is incompatible with the religion of technological and material progress.

So our young head out into the world uninitiated. Desper-ately, some of them do their best to self-initiate, getting involved with alcohol or drugs, fast cars and reckless be-haviour, or they end up falling head-first into some ideo-logy that promises clear rules in an unclear world of fuzzy and manipulated narratives. As a result, many of them end up dead with a needle in their arm, bleeding their life out in the twisted remains of a mangled car or as cannon fod-der for ariel bombers on some dusty and distant battle-field.

The real tragedy, it seems to me, is that we can't recognise how readily we abandon our young, how unquestioningly we push them out into the void with no other guidance about life other than 'study hard and get a well-paid job'. Effectively we are telling them that the world is dead and that, by extension, nothing matters other than their own shallow material satisfaction. Is it any wonder that some of them develop a nihilistic world view and grow up to be shallow weak-minded consumers or tortured souls?

This, when I dwell upon it, bothers me, for what is to be-come of a society that abandons wisdom, puts the theoret-ical above the experiential and tells its young that there is no point in living? Raising a child to adulthood should be

101

a sacred duty and one that we forsake at our peril. We have forsaken it. We are now in peril. We have developed generations of stunted adults.

Many people are cut off from the natural world that we depend on to survive. They are all too willing to destroy it for the sake of short term economic gain or comfort. But what are we to do if we recognise this as so? How can we self-initiate to reconnect? Perhaps we just need to get ourselves back into nature, throw open the doors to the channels of perception and see what happens.

Chapter 12. Our Faustian pact

"What do I think of Western civilisation? I think it would be a very good idea."

– Gandhi

The next day, and the one after that, I spent walking around in the forest. As I walked I beat out the rhythm of my progress with the wooden staff. Every two seconds or so it would touch down on the leafy trail at an angle of about seventy degrees. I would walk two or three steps and the staff's angle would open up to about one hundred and twenty degrees before I lifted it, swung it forward and repeated. I did mental arithmetic as I beat out this meditative march. With each staff fall, I calculated, we burned through two thousand barrels of oil. With each staff fall eight people were born and four people died. With each staff fall unpayable global debt rose by some unfathomable figure.

Then one day it rained so much that all the trails turned into streams and so I put off my walking and sat in the cabin with my diary. The thoughts I had been having over the previous couple of days poured forth from my pen. My presence in the forest had cleared my mind and I decided to write a diary entry that I could later turn into a post on my blog:

Given the reality that the quality of our energy supplies is diminishing, combined with the fact that the number of people who have a claim on those supplies is growing every day, it should be clear to see that the amount of energy available to us individually is going to lessen with each passing day. The best then that we can hope for is a transition to a situation where we are able to live with renewable forms of energy that permit us some conveniences but don't destroy the climate in the process.

Such a transition will be far from easy. We have lived through the Age of Plenty and the Age of More and it remains an unknown as to how we will adapt to the Age of Less. At the level of society things do not bode well. Psychologists know that the pain people experience when things are taken away from them is greater than the happiness they experienced when acquiring it. Perhaps this is because we are an acquisitive species, or perhaps it is simply that we are unable to let go. Whatever the reason, it seems clear that people collectively will do everything they can to hold onto the comfortable illusion that the Age of Plenty can continue unabated.

But nature, as they say, bats last. And nature cares not for the whims and ambitions of humankind so, as the remorseless march of resource exploitation continues apace on our small and delicate planet those who recognise this fact may have the better chance of adapting to the new reality. In the case of the industrial economies into which we have been born, the prognosis for survival looks dim. Our society has become a resource-hungry beast that requires ever greater growth just to survive. Key components of it, namely the military, the industrial complex and the research institutions which provide it with fresh young recruits, have become merged and they consume the lion's share of the resources.

Were any of these to be suddenly starved of energy or credit the likely cascading collapse scenario would draw a line under industrial civilisation as a whole, marking the end of this particular chapter in the human journey. Yet given that industrial civilisation requires growth without end, irrespective of planetary limitations, it is inevitable that it will fail at some point. The fact that this point is being reached during our lifetimes is simply our bad luck. We have no choice but to deal with it.

Any in-depth study of history will reveal patterns of expansion and contraction, usually marked by the rise and fall of empires or civilisations. The German historian and philosopher Oswald Spengler spent much of his life analysing civilisations – their blossoming, their decay and eventual downfall. Most of us are familiar with various past civilisations such as the Hellenic Greeks, the Romans, the Maya and the Egyptians, but there are dozens more of which we know comparatively little and the last time I checked they were not teaching many school kids about the ancient Guptas, Toltecs or Sumerians. Spengler identified Western European civilisation, from which the industrial revolution was born, as essentially a Faustian one, and one that has been in steady decline for around a hundred years already.

This might seem like a strange thought to most. Aren't we led to believe that 'we' are the pinnacle of human achievement and that history's arrow points only in the direction of ever greater technical achievement until, one day, we will find ourselves spread out throughout the galaxy? This way of thinking, which could be called progressive, permeates our popular culture and tempts us to consider what glories lie in our collective future. Things are getting better, we are told, and if they are not then it's because the government (or some other human organisation) is inept or corrupt.

This, at least, is the official story. In Goethe's mystic work Doctor Faustus, the eponymous character sold his soul to the devil in return for the deep knowledge that would unlock the mysteries of the universe and provide him with power over his fellow men. He signs the deal with Lucifer in his own blood and is immediately able to enjoy great powers, such as the ability to make himself invisible. With this trickery he is able to cause mischief in all the great courts of Europe and beyond. In all, he enjoys twenty-four years of power, but as the end draws near he becomes full of the fear of death as he knows he will soon have to pay his half of the bargain. He repents, but it is too late, and his soul is dragged howling down to hell.

105

Doctor Faustus is quite a morality tale, but in terms of our energy and climate predicaments such morality tales are not particularly useful other than as a scholarly footnote in future history books. What is useful to understand however is that, if Spengler, Goethe, Einstein and a whole host of others are correct, then as the day of reckoning for our industrial civilisation grows closer it will not serve us well to continue to try making deals with Lucifer to extend it. More technology and modernity is leading to more, not fewer, problems stored up for us. And wasn't the whole point of science and technology to solve our problems?

It is here that we should consider the possibility that new technologies may in fact be traps. That by solving one problem we lay the foundations of a newer, bigger, problem further down the road. Thus, the chemical fertiliser revolution which led to an explosion in the number of people living in the arid lands of north Africa and the Middle East now leads to the spectre of mass famine and völkerwanderung. To combat this we are told that genetically modified rice will be needed to improve yields. For the sake of argument, let's assume that genetically modified rice was a success and that it allowed the numbers to swell by another half. What then? Inevitably we would need to find another planet to support our burgeoning numbers. And then another, and another.

But nature is not going to supply us with another planet, no matter how shrilly people insist that it will. It has taken us several billion years to evolve on this one, and the chances of our being able to survive on another one are vanishingly slim. Not that we would ever be able to reach another planet without some equally improbable harnessing of quantum physics. Even if we were able to locate an exact replica of Earth, given our current best technology for space travel – a craft that can travel at around 35,000mph – it would take us at least a quarter of a million years to travel the thirteen light years to the nearest likely planetary neighbourhood.

Given that all of recorded human history at best occupies six or seven thousand years, the chances of us surviving 250,000 in a space ship would seem rather slim. Even then, the chances of any planet being habitable are almost infinitely remote – we might find that the next suitable rock is another billion years or so away in our somewhat beaten-up old rocket ship. In the light of these considerations betting on being able to relocate to another planet doesn't seem like such a good idea after all.

All of which is to say that we'll have to relearn how to survive on the planet we evolved to live on, without the benefit of such a wasteful industrial system. This might sound like a tall order, but it's the only choice we have. Our ancestors managed it quite well, and were even getting rather good at not just surviving but living in comfort with what nature provided. Until fossil fuels came along and torpedoed the project.

Consider the fact that the Romans had central heating systems, that ancient toilets have been unearthed in Jerusalem and that extensive ocean going trading routes existed up the west coast of Europe. The Spaniards conquered the Americas without the benefit of a single drop of oil and the ancient civilisations of Egypt had alchemists capable of producing clocks, batteries and radios. Ancient Greece even saw the first robot in the form of a steam-powered mechanical pigeon.

None of these cultures had access to the phenomenal amounts of fossil fuels we have, neither did they suffer under the immense complexities that are now beginning to drag us down – yet that didn't stop them from being civilisations worth living in. Indeed, looking at the great sweep of history, recorded or otherwise, we can see that what we currently consider as normal is far from it.

But fossil fuels are going away and our big challenge is to leave as much of them in the ground as possible. As they ebb away so too does the complexity of our techno-indus-trial civilisation. One of the biggest problems that our des-cendants will face for the next few thousand years is the problem of radiation from stricken nuclear reactors, be-cause as civilisational complexity lessens, so too does our ability to handle the dangerous chains of events that we have set in progress. It is likely that in the future, large zones of irradiated land and sea will be set aside as unin-habitable while the radioactive elements slowly decay over many thousands of years.

The second, probably more immediate, problem we face stems directly from our lack of petroleum. Previous civil-isations, despite their differences in religious beliefs, so-cial organisation and culture, tended to be agrarian in nature. We, however, rely on cheap oil to power a planet-spanning network of supply chains that deliver food to our plates in a just-in-time manner. Local knowledge of food production has in many cases gone the way of the dodo and even most farmers – those who are charged with sup-plying us with nutritious food – are slaves to the system and wholly addicted to the synthetic products it supplies.

Furthermore, due to the application of these synthetic products, most of the topsoil in the world is degraded and barren. Often it is little more than a substrate in which to prop up plants. Modern soil is a lifeless, nutrient free crumble of chemical additives that is more or less useless to other lifeforms. If, in the UK, all oil and chemical fertil-isers and pesticides were taken away overnight, it is doubt-ful that we could feed even a quarter of the population. The last time we were ever remotely tested in this respect was during the Second World War. We just about managed it then, but since then much of the countryside has been concreted over, valuable farming skills have been lost, ploughing animals scarcely exist, soil quality has de-graded markedly and there are twice as many mouths to feed.

Yet without the gargantuan energy subsidies the techno-logy industry relies upon, the economies of scale will not be there to produce much in the way of high-tech goods and medicines. Although some claim that we have effect-ively 'ephemeralised' our way of life – pointing out that an iPhone today has more computing power than a main-frame computer from thirty years ago and yet is a fraction of the size and weight – are missing the point. The sprawl-ing factories, international supply lines and money gob-bling educational institutions needed to make that iPhone occupy much more space and take up far more energy than that old dusty mainframe spooling out its reams of paper. As the energy and credit feed-lines are cut, high tech ceases to be able to pay its way in the world, forcing us to simplify the way in which we live our lives and conduct our business. And there lies the problem.

I put down my ranting pen. It's hard being a Cassandra sometimes. Why should I care about these things in any case? Most other people seemed to be able to avoid think-ing about them, so why – for the sake of an easy life – couldn't I? For that I had no answer. Perhaps some are just hard-wired to dwell upon paradox.

Chapter 13. Reflections on a lake

"Happy is the man who has broken the chains which hurt the mind, and has given up worrying once and for all."

– Ovid

It was the middle of the night and I awoke suddenly, my eyes flicking open. I lay there for a few minutes wondering why I was awake. Outside it was silent and still. There was no rain. I unzipped the tent and peered out. The sky was clear and the moon was high in the sky, illuminating the forest with its soft cold light. Without really knowing why, I pulled on my clothes and stepped out. I walked silently through the campsite and over the empty road. The small lake where the swans lived seemed to beckon me and I felt myself being drawn towards its shore. There I sat and watched the reflection of the moon on its silky surface. And as the moon reflected so too did I. I thought about the chapter of *Soulcraft* I had been reading before I had fallen asleep. It had been about knowing yourself, and recognising that there is more than one of you.

Who am I? I thought. Certainly there is the intrinsic 'me' that we reference when we think of ourselves – but is that all? No, it turns out – we are made up of a whole host of characters. These sub-personalities are all there inside us. The ego – that which we see as 'I' – is just one of them, although usually it is the one with the loudest voice. Who else lies within? Our five year-old selves are certainly there, as are our teenage selves. Each of these holds all the joys and sorrows, the fears and wonder that we experienced and felt as we passed through these ages, and often their voices can still be heard in the rabble of our mind. Maybe we have a go-getting twenty-something sub-personality in there, and a wiser, older seventy year-old whom we have not yet become. They are all in there, living side by side within us.

And then there is, as Bill Plotkin calls it, the 'loyal soldier'. This sub-personality is like the Japanese soldiers from the second world war who wound up on remote Pacific islands, only to be discovered decades later still believing that the war was raging. Numerous actual cases of Japanese soldiers have been found in this way, and it has been very difficult to make them believe that the war actually ended many years before (and that they lost). Can you imagine taking one of these soldiers and, upon returning him to civilisation, instead of putting him in a care home with understanding staff, he were given a job at the top level of government?

One can easily imagine that, if such a thing were to happen, his every policy recommendation would involve conflict and starting new wars of vengeance. Yet each of us has our own loyal soldier inside who has fought valiantly to protect us from psychological harm during the formative years of our lives, but who is no longer needed now we have grown into mature adults. Maybe we need to learn to retire our loyal soldiers from active duty, and stop electing them into places of leadership.

Within us all there are male and female sub-personalities, each with their own very different attributes that, put together, form a whole. This has little to do with actual gender but everything to do with tendencies to act and think. The masculine likes to measure, gather and control things, whereas the feminine likes to nurture, nourish and grow.

Then we have the soul. Some say that we are not bodies with souls, but souls with bodies. But what is it? We know that in our modern society we repress the soul at all costs, pandering instead to the clutching ego or the fearful loyal soldier sub-personality. But the soul is buoyant, like a cork, wanting to rise up and become re-connected again with the greater spirit or cosmos. Perhaps, as is suggested by many, the true purpose of life is to set your soul free to

111

become connected with the greater whole again, thus reflecting the brilliance of creation. Instead many of us have become disconnected and dull-minded, like dirty mirrors in a dusty old shop.

Sub-personalities and soul elements aside, there are others among us that are not 'us'. Consider this:

The human microbiome is the aggregate of microorganisms, a microbiome that resides on the surface and in deep layers of skin, in the saliva and oral mucosa, in the conjunctiva, and in the gastrointestinal tracts. They include bacteria, fungi, and archaea. One study indicated they outnumber human cells 10 to 1. Some of these organisms perform tasks that are useful for the human host. However, the majority have been too poorly researched for us to understand the role they play, however communities of microflora have been shown to change their behaviour in diseased individuals. – Wikipedia

We are, in fact, whole ecosystems. Bacteria have evolved to live alongside and within us over billions of years. Our immune systems are comprised of armies of organisms that possess their own intelligence, working on our behalf to attack unwelcome viruses. They work relentlessly to repel alien invaders and, when they eventually give up the ghost, so do we. How do we treat these exquisite ecosystems that have stood us in such good stead? We feed them with food laced with pesticides and other chemicals, bludgeon them with legal and illegal drugs and put pseudo foods such as Max burgers down our throats.

And yet, instead of recognising the multitude of sub-psychic personalities and the communities of different organisms that comprise us, it seems that we have chosen a path of atomisation and separation. We are at war with ourselves. And if we are at war with ourselves how can we ever hope to stop waging war on the wider biosphere? We have created a system of politics that caters to the worst type of our personalities, putting everything in opposition with itself.

I cast my mind back to the COP15 climate conference that took place in Copenhagen in 2009. It was anticipated that this would be the moment when climate change went mainstream, and the various environmental groups had hoped that leadership from the top would finally be forthcoming after decades of trying to ignore the problem. At the time I was producing a newspaper to cover the conference and was closely connected with all that was going on there.

Towards the end, after two weeks of sideshows, the US president Barack Obama was due to meet with the Chinese premier Wen Jiabao in the hope of making a deal to protect future generations from climate chaos. One would have hoped that these two powerful men – human inhabitants of planet Earth – would be able to seize their moment in history and steer us away from the hard brick wall of ecological limits towards which we are accelerating. Perhaps they would have the wisdom to see what a child could intuitively tell them; that we are damaging our world to such an extent that it may soon become uninhabitable.

Alas, no such wisdom was forthcoming. The two sides were like warlords, each arriving in a huge airplane like conquering chiefs, and surrounded by legions of cold-faced officials whose job it was to advise and make sure that everything was in their narrow range of interest. The atmosphere was tense, almost violent, and neither side was willing to budge in defending its 'right' to continue to burn up the planet's store of hydrocarbons, even if it meant death and untold misery for billions.

So it goes.

Imagine, instead, if the two men had arrived and were immediately escorted away from their teams of advisors. Imagine that they had been transported to some remote wilderness area of great beauty and stripped of their status, their phones and computers and everything else that gave them power. That they were given simple robes and ample but comfortable accommodation in a setting of peace and serenity, perhaps overlooking lakes and mountains, and that all of their meals were simple and nutritious, and that these meals were brought to them by children each day. Imagine that every day they would sit beside a fire and hear tales of wisdom from native elders and watch dance performances and share their inner stories.

Then, after some period of days or weeks, the two men would get down to business and talk about their own hopes and fears for the future, their children and all the disappointments and upsets they had experienced in life. They would focus on how, using their great gift of power, they could work to heal the damage, both inner and outer, that was causing so many problems within the world. Imagine then that this was the setting for their negotiations to commence.

Get real.

Any suggestion that politics could be conducted in the above manner would be met with howls of derision by the 'realists'. Those in the top positions of government and corporations are there because they are good at climbing the structures of power at the expense of others. Perhaps it is not even possible to reform them as individuals, so practiced are they in the Machiavellian arts.

Our system of politics and governance does not allow for wisdom to prevail. It is instead hardwired for conflict and war, both against one another and against the planet, and the people it is supposed to represent are trapped like slaves within the system and unable to imagine better ways of doing things. It is because we have allowed the so-called realists and rationalists to prevail that we have allowed our one home in the universe to be poisoned and abused.

If we are to turn this situation around it will be the job of the new generations of people to re-connect with the sacred, re-assemble the human mind and re-birth a new form of consciousness that will replace the disconnected con-

sciousness that now threatens the very fabric of our existence. Whether this will be possible is really the biggest
question there is. But I know that for such a thing to happen it will have to occur one person at a time and that humanity may have to endure a near-death experience to
shock us into action. I felt sure that such a shock was coming, and soon.

These were the thoughts that passed through my mind as I
sat quietly in the moonlight beside that Swedish lake.

Chapter 14. Talking to trees

"*Trees are sanctuaries. Whoever knows how to speak to them, whoever knows how to listen to them, can learn the truth... Trees have long thoughts, long-breathing and restful, just as they have longer lives than ours. They are wiser than we are, as long as we do not listen to them... Whoever has learned how to listen to trees no longer wants to be a tree. He wants to be nothing except what he is. That is home. That is happiness.*"

– Herman Hesse, *Bäume. Betrachtungen und Gedichte* (*Trees. Reflections and Poems*)

One day I thought: why not talk to a tree? After all, people talk to their computers all the time. They howl at their TV screens when they show something they don't agree with and they chastise their cars when they break down. If we can talk to machines without any sense of irony then why not trees? We share plenty of genes with trees. As a matter of fact we have a single common ancestor and some of our DNA is identical to that of an oak tree. There is wood in our bones and sap in our blood. What's more, trees have been around a lot longer than we humans, so is it such a stretch of the imagination to consider that they too may have evolved means of communication?

The first thing to recognise about trees is that they are up-side down. At least from our point of view. Given that I'm a human and you're a human then this is a shared point of view. Trees effectively have their brains – in this case the root system – buried under the ground. Their legs, which are thrust up into the air, and their many feet and toes possess a magical ability to grow miniature solar panels each year which they then use to deliver energy to their mind, body and spirit. We call them leaves. When winter comes these solar panels drop to the ground to be assimilated back into the substrate that surrounds the tree's 'brain'. Consider this:

"For their neural networks to function, plants use virtually the same neurotransmitters we do, including the two most important: glutamate and GABA (gamma amino butyric acid). They also utilize, as do we, acetylcholine, dopamine, serotonin, melatonin, epinephrine, norepinephrine, levodopa, indole-3-acetic acid, 5-hydroxyindole acetic acid, testosterone (and other androgens), estradiol (and other estrogens), nicotine, and a number of other neuroactive compounds. They also make use of their plant-specific neurotransmitter, auxin, which, like serotonin, for example, is synthesised from tryptophan. These transmitters are used, as they are in us, for communication within the organism and to enhance brain function." – Stephen H Buhner, *Plant Intelligence and the Imaginal Realm*

So it seems that plants, such as trees, and humans have a lot in common. As primates we spent most of our evolutionary journey high up in the branches of trees and we have evolved to be able to eat many of their fruits and nuts. That's why we can eat chocolate and dogs cannot. But trees are much older than us, having been on Earth for some three hundred and eighty five million years, when they appeared as toilet brush-like plants with woody stems rising up eight metres into the air.

These primitive trees, which first appeared close to where modern day New York City is situated, were called *cladoxylopsids*, and they could harvest sunlight using photosynthesis. In the wake of their appearance the first forest ecosystems began to spread around the planet. Shortly thereafter another form of tree began to emerge and it would look far more familiar to our eyes. The *archaeopteris* was a large shrub that looked something like a conifer. It grew to thirty metres in height and its deep roots allowed for biomass to build up and for life to flourish around it.

Given that they had hard woody stems that grew taller and

thicker rather than dying back every winter, these early trees could remove large amounts of CO_2 from the atmosphere. In combination with the oxygen they exhaled, the changes to the Earth's climate were profound, with CO_2 levels dropping by up to ninety five percent. This period is known to us as the carboniferous and the remains of the trees from this stage of the Earth's evolution are still with us in the form of coal. Large flat leaves began to appear around that time and trees evolved to produce seeds rather than relying on wind pollination.

Something extraordinary happened about three hundred million years ago. A cataclysmic earthquake caused an entire section of forest to suddenly sink down below sea level whereupon it was instantly swamped. Over the aeons these interred trees slowly turned into coal and today we can see them underground in Illinois, if one ventures down the Vermillion Grove coal mine. Since the seam of coal lying below the subterranean forest has been mined out, it is possible to go down beneath this ancient preserved ecosystem and gaze up at the roots of immense fossilised trees from a lost world. These trees have been hidden inside the planet's crust for a third of a billion years, still possessing their original form. Amongst the specimens here are immense tree-like club mosses, growing up to forty metres in length and unlike anything recognisable in today's world.

These trees had already been around for some two hundred and twenty million years by the time we got around to evolving from tree shrews. We spent the next forty-odd million years scampering around in the branches as monkeys and it wasn't until relatively recently that the first hominid appeared, about fifteen million years ago. Halve that time again and we branch off from the common ancestor we share with chimpanzees, and halve it once more to get to *australopithecus afarensis* – the most well-known example of which is Lucy – who finally seems to have come down from the trees to hunt and scavenge on the plains of east Africa about three million years ago.

So, given that approximately ninety six percent of our evolutionary journey from tree shrew to industrialised *homo sapiens* has been spent in the trees, is it too much to wonder that we may have co-evolved some kind of shared communication channel? I decided to find out.

I walked out along the plateau on the southern side of the gorge and stepped off the path into an area I had not explored before. I wanted to get lost. Not seriously lost, but lost enough that I could not find my bearings. I figured that this mental state of low-level anxiety would help suppress the controlling ego part of my mind which is said to be unconducive to the reception of messages from the plant world in a similar way that sitting beside a screaming toddler is unconducive to focusing on hushed Gregorian chanting. To further heighten the senses I abstained from eating anything for the day and headed out at dusk.

When I considered myself sufficiently lost I began to look around for a likely tree to communicate with. Beech trees may all look fairly alike when seen in the aggregate, but when you are up close to them and trying to decide which one might look friendly enough to talk with then they all begin to look very different. Some of them seemed to have faces. There were long, grimacing faces with bulging features, Pinocchio noses, Picasso eyes and ghastly mouths like something from an Edvard Munch painting, and there were faces that looked altogether more benign, if somewhat misshapen and ugly. I tried to put prejudices aside – after all, I reasoned, perhaps I looked equally gruesome to them.

Nevertheless, as I moved between the trees I attempted to get a feeling for each of them, gauging whether any caused a particular sensation within me. I didn't want to talk to an unfriendly tree – after all, if one is truly open-minded about the possibility that they may be as intelligent as we are, that they possess characters traits, talents and foibles, then one must not discount the possibility that some of them may be bastards.

It wasn't too long before I saw a friendly-looking tree. It was a medium sized one, probably about the same age as myself. I had discounted talking with any of the truly immense trees with their huge trunks and their gnarled roots. Perhaps I was intimidated by their size. In any case, I went up to this particular tree and introduced myself. It felt a bit strange talking to a tree, but there were no people around in this off-the-track part of the forest, so why should I feel embarrassed? I was not naive enough to expect a pair of woody eyes to flick open and for the tree to start talking to me like one of Tolkein's ents, nevertheless I talked in a spirit of openness. I told it who I was, where I came from and what was important to me. Bill Plotkin states that trees are not interested in names or other types of human categorisation, so I outlined myself in terms of the heart. This is not as easy as it sounds, given how used we are to describing ourselves in terms that would look okay on a CV. Trying to describe yourself in terms that you think a non-human plant organism will understand is a useful way of evaluating your place in the biophysical world.

After a while I had run out of things to say so I sat down at the base of the tree and rummaged in my bag. I had brought a gift for it, as was advised by Plotkin – in this case a very large and very red rosehip from a bush near the campsite. There were no rose bushes in the deep forest because of the lack of light, so I figured it might make a reasonable gift. I placed the hip in a bole formed by the tree's roots that looked a bit like a natural shrine. After I had done this I sat and waited. I waited for about twenty minutes or so and then shifted position so that I sat with my back against the trunk. I meditated for a bit to try and clear my mind of unwanted background noise.

One thing that I was aware of was that trees could be much more leisurely with their communication than we humans. In *Soulcraft* Bill Plotkin describes one of his wilderness soul questers talking to a desert tree for several days, asking how it managed to survive in such an arid desert. The tree had remained silent and seemingly aloof for the whole time. Eventually the seeker became exasperated and started shouting at it, upon which the tree bellowed back "Deep roots!". The inquisitor was bowled over in shock.

But I didn't have several days to spend waiting, so my hopes of pulling off an inter-species conversation weren't awfully high. Nevertheless, I persisted and carried on talking. I talked about my own bit of woodland in Cornwall, describing the various trees to be found there and talking about how I was planting many more with each passing year. As I was doing so I felt an almost imperceptible change of something in the air. It felt as if the tree were actually listening to me. "Go on", it seemed to say when I paused. The hairs on my arms stood on end.

And so I carried on, talking about the land and the trees, and how I had come to be in this forest and that soon I would be leaving it again, probably never to return. I repeated various points several times, trying to tune into the feelings I was getting back from the tree. I had probably been there for about an hour by this stage and was wondering whether I was just imagining things. I wanted to know if this was the case or not and so I asked the tree to give me a sign that it was listening to me. I awaited a response, somewhat fearfully.

Fearfully? Fearfully because if it's true that plants and trees are sentient beings with an advanced state of intelligence then the terrible things we humans are doing to them in forests around the world just got even more terrible. Indeed, I myself was no stranger to chainsaws, having cut down about two hundred trees the previous winter in my woodland for coppice. So I gulped and waited for a response. And there it was. Thud. I looked down at the ground. There, beside my foot, was a large nut cupule. I picked it and examined it. There were four nuts there, healthy and ripe.

I was astonished. All morning I had been looking for beech seeds to take back with me, but despite the millions of husks lying around on the forest floor they had all been empty, no doubt eaten by birds and rodents. This was the first one I had seen with actual seeds in it. I looked up at the tree and thanked it. I would take the seeds back home and germinate them, and within a couple of years I hoped they would be good strong seedlings growing in my woodland. "Good", the tree seemed to say. I bid it farewell and walked back to the path, which didn't take too long to find, clutching the seeds in my hand.

Was I going mad? Quite possibly, I concluded. But perhaps, as the sixth great extinction takes hold, climate chaos picks up pace and people run around cutting off other people's heads in the name of their god, just perhaps it is the mad ones who are the sane ones in this topsy turvy world.

Chapter 15: Woodlander

"One of the first conditions of happiness is that the link between Man and Nature shall not be broken."

– Leo Tolstoy

On a whim one day when the sun was out, I left the path and struck out into the forest along what I considered to be a straight trajectory. In my experience, the few hikers I encountered rarely left the track and I thought that perhaps I would stumble across some more burial mounds or abandoned settlements. I walked for about half an hour, taking care to keep looking around for markers and gauging where the sun was from time to time. The forest became denser but then it opened out into a series of glades. One of them was illuminated by beams of dappled sunlight, making the grass and the feathery moss appear bright green. It was a scene straight from the pages of a book of fairy tales and I couldn't resist entering the glade and stretching out on the moss. Looking up, I felt the rays of the sun gently warm my face as the faint whisper of a breeze stirred the leaves in the trees around me.

As I lay there I thought of my own piece of woodland, a thousand miles to the west, and how I liked to lie in the sun there during the heat of summer. It had been an abrupt change of lifestyle, from working in an office to working as a woodsman, and I was still getting to grips with it. The wood comprises seven acres of oak and sweet chestnut coppice situated on the side of a shallow valley in west Cornwall. On still summer evenings you can hear the waves breaking on the beach two miles away as the crow flies, and gaze at the stars in the dark skies above. I had bought the woodland as a refuge. It was a place of safety and sanity and it could provide me with half an income in the form of wood products and charcoal.

The first winter I cut down a half acre of chestnut. Because none of the trees were older than twenty five they were still manageable for one man, and no heavy machinery was needed. The trees began to grow back the following spring, shooting up new growth from the smoothly cut stumps, and the newly-exposed forest floor became a carpet of wildflowers. The next winter I coppiced another, smaller, area, with the idea being that a twelve year rotational plan would give me a sustainable means of making money in a way that used to be widely practiced in Britain, but which had fallen by the wayside since the advent of the fossil fuel age.

And the woodland, if listened to and managed correctly, is transforming into a haven for wildlife and biodiversity. As I work in my woodland I respect the land around me. I do not 'own' the land in any deeper sense than merely possessing papers that name me as its legal owner. I am merely passing through, doing what I can to heal the damage that centuries of poor management have done to it. It used to be a part of a rich family's country estate and it had been given over to sheep and cow farming since as far back as the records tell. Much of the land is steep and, for this reason, about a quarter of a century ago, it was decided to plant most of it up with chestnut coppice. Chestnut wood, known for its strength and its ability to hold off rot in damp conditions, was for many years used for tunnel bracing by the miners at the neighbouring Poldark mine, and it has a long association with Cornwall. As the land turned from pasture to woodland the landed gentry, and high-paying foreign businessmen, used it as a place to shoot pheasants, so I am told, although today none of the game birds remain.

As I work the land I make sure that I give as much as I can back to nature. Dead wood is stacked to provide homes for insects and bees. Flowers and weeds are mostly left to do their thing, and I am convinced that by allowing nature to grow feral and wild, the various species of plant, insect, fungi and animal will be able to create a natural order far better than can I. I am always mindful of the fact that I am but one creature among thousands there, even if I do have the power to modify the woodland to suit my own needs, so I try to avoid behaving like an ecological dictator. I am working to improve the land too. A large pond has been dug by hand and hundreds of broad-leaf trees have been planted on former pasture that had become compacted and degraded. I am aiming for maximum biodiversity, and in summer the woodland is aflutter with butterflies and abuzz with bees. There is nothing I like doing better than sitting in the long grass beneath an elder tree, watching the lives of the birds and the insects. Maybe they are watching me back.

In her remarkable book *Wild*, Jay Griffiths writes about walking in forests in sensual terms. One goes *into* a forest, she says, and notes that most indigenous cultures regard forests as female entities. She goes further, quoting Freud. "All of these dark woods, narrow defiles, high grounds and deep penetrations are unconscious sexual imagery, and we are exploring a woman's body." One who loves forests is known as a *nemophile*, from the Greek *nemos*, meaning wooded grove, and *philia*, meaning to love. Haunting the wooded groves in awed reverence is therefore an act of *nemophilia*.

It has only been with the advent of the world's monotheist revealed religions that the forests, stripped of their divine femininity, have become dark and threatening places in the popular imagination. In the eyes of the Church these earthy green places were full of chaos, disorder and pagan desires. As such they were only good for chopping down or turning into pasture. Those who still dwell in the world's last remaining forests believe otherwise. Amazonian Indians, for example, know that the forest sustains them and that, without it, they cannot live. In fact, they see the entire Amazon rainforest as a benign protector, a divine female who brings forth life, and regard it as hotbed of lusty fecundity.

By contrast, our view of forests is usually set down in terms of their economic value. In Britain, when one looks at woodlands advertised for sale the talk is usually of how much timber can be extracted and what price it can fetch on the market. Even when aesthetic considerations trump economic value, forests are often only considered worth hanging onto for their pleasant appearance, and they are rarely permitted to become too wild or unruly, or – God forbid – inaccessible. Cut down to size, we thus talk about woodlots, management plans and extraction rates. Men go into forests with lethal toys to kill the animals and de-wild them. They pose with their kills with Facebook grins, thinking themselves real men. The abuse of the world's forests is so widespread and ingrained that it is difficult to escape the conclusion that we have a deep-seated hatred of them – a hatred that acts as a mask for a fear of what we do not understand.

I don't know if I actually fell asleep thinking about my woodland and my relationship to it but after what seemed like only a short while I felt a nearby presence. With the crack of a twig and the rustle of leaves I sat up and looked around. I half expected to find myself catching a browsing deer unawares but instead I realised that it was I who had been discovered. A man, whiskery and somewhat pot-bellied, was standing nearby and regarding me. He was wearing a faded Rage Against the Machine t-shirt and, in his hand, he held a large wicker basket overflowing with mushrooms.

It was the same man I had seen in the forest a few days before when I followed the fox; the one who had ignored me when I'd said hello. I looked at him and he looked back at me and then he put a finger up to his lips and said "*Shhhh!*". And with that he walked slowly out of the glade and continued with his foraging. I had to laugh. Collecting mushrooms was strictly forbidden according to the park literature, even though there were over one and half thousand different types of fungus growing here.

Who'd begrudge this man of the forest his basket of mush-rooms? Certainly not I.

Chapter 16. Into the gash

"We all have forests on our minds. Forests unexplored, unending. Each one of us gets lost in the forest, every night, alone."

– Ursula Le Guin, *The Wind's Twelve Quarters*

In the middle of the night I awoke to hear a storm raging. The rain was hammering down outside and the occasional flicker of lightning lit up the inside of the tent. I was dry on my patch of sand under the roof but I had the sensation that the whole area was drowning under the sheer assault of the rain. I fell asleep once more and when morning came I became aware of a heavy moist warmth, as if the tent had become a sauna. I peered outside and saw clear blue skies and little evidence of the storm in the night. On the wet grass beside the children's swings some little grey-feathered wagtails hopped around and looked at me expectantly. I reached inside the tent and pulled out a piece of baguette, throwing them a few crumbs. The birds inspected my offering critically before judging it inedible, instead flying off to a patch of long grass to hunt for less alien foodstuffs.

I lay there and enjoyed the warmth. In the night, after the storm, I had had another of my flying dreams. This had been a recurring dream every now and again for the last few years and it involved being on a plane that was flying close to the ground. The details of the dream usually changed, but some aspects were always the same. The plane was always a large jumbo jet and it was always flying close to the ground – so close, in fact, that it seemed we were skimming over the tops of trees, houses and rock formations. In the dream I was alarmed by the plane's proximity to the ground but couldn't express my fear.

Whenever I tried to speak my mouth seized up and all I could make were muffled sounds. The other passengers either ignored me or assured me there was no danger. For some reason the destination of my dream planes was always New York, although 'New York' was sometimes a canyon, a forest or the rocky side of a mountain. In one memorable dream I was flying through a canyon and the tips of the wings were inches from the rock walls as the hostesses smiled and served drinks.

I didn't know why I was having these dreams or whether they meant anything in particular. I wasn't particularly worried by flying in my conscious state, and the planes never actually crashed in the dreams, although I had woken up screaming on several occasions as I believed we were about to collide with mountains or trees. I lay there and tried to recall the details of the dream, but they slipped from sight as my conscious self took over, retreating into the shadows of my mind.

I went inside the hut to put on some coffee and make myself a bowl of muesli. The hut felt like a sanctuary and, over the last few days, I had found that I was usually the only person in it except for those few campers using the shower facilities. There was a television on the wall but I had resisted the urge to turn it on. I had not checked what was going on in the wider world for about a week and had no urge to do so. The news seemed somewhat irrelevant to me, and I was quite happy not to indulge it. Today, I decided, I would descend into the gorge. So far on my walks around the forest I had only explored the beech forests that covered the upper reaches on the plateau above the gorge. Down in the gorge, I had read, the ecosystem had remained mostly undisturbed by people. The prospect of walking there intrigued me.

On the wall in the cabin was a picture of a small frozen lake ringed with trees beneath an azure blue sky. The whole scene was frosted in snow and I knew that this must be the Odin's Lake the woman in the tourist office in

Malmö had told me about. I gazed for a while at the picture. I had seen hundreds of images of picturesque Swedish lakes but there seemed to be something alluring about this particular one. Perhaps it was what the tourist brochures said, that a cult of the god Odin had flourished there and maybe this explained the lake's magnetic pull.

As I finished my breakfast I mused on this, the kernel of an idea forming in my mind. I washed up my breakfast dishes and walked across the silent highway to the yellow house where Björn lived. I had seen he had a copy of a glossy book about the national park and I wanted to find out more about the lake. He wasn't in when I got there but he had given me the key code for the door so I opened it and went in. The floorboards of the house creaked as I walked across the lounge and sat myself down in a wooden rocking chair with the book. I found the page about Odin's Lake and read it.

The Odensjö lake is an almost circular lake near Röstånga in the southern part of the national park. The lake gets its water solely from ground water and rain... The depth of water in the lake is about 20 metres; this is followed by a thick layer of sediment and mud to a depth of 24 metres where boulders are met. It is probably very deep, perhaps 60 metres down to firm rock, as fallen material from the lake's sides also covers the lake's floor.

The geologists seemed to have done a good job of measuring the dimensions of the lake, but when it came to agreeing on how it was formed they were not so sure, as the next paragraph explained.

Many theories have been put forward about how the Odensjö lake was formed and even today geologists are not certain. For a long time it was believed that it was the remains of a volcano, but there are no volcanic rock types in the area. For many decades the theory that the lake and the fault valleys had been made deeper by an enormous waterfall from the ice in a so-called catastrophic emptying was popular, but that theory was rejected as there are no

130

large erosion deposits at the valley's outlet. The latest theory is that the Odensjö lake was formed as a so-called niche glacier.

As for attributing any supernatural qualities to the lake the guidebook pours glacial meltwater on such suggestions.

Odensjön was first written as Odensjö in 1729 but it is understood today to be a completely invented mythical name emanating from fantasies about the lake's dramatic topography and wild nature. It is believed that people previously wrongly interpreted [the name] Onsjö judicial district as 'Odensjö' – a cult place for the Norse god Odin – but the district did not get its name from either the god or the lake.

Reading that, I wondered how the writer could be so sure that the peoples of ancient Scania did not use the lake as a place of worship for their god of wisdom. I found a more romantic explanation for the lake's name on a leaflet put out by the local regional tourist board:

Hidden away in the Nackarpsdalen valley in Röstånga, surrounded by 30-metre high precipices, you can find the circular lake of Odensjön (Odin's Lake). According to folklore in tales of old, there lies an air of mystery over this lake. The formation of the lake remains an enigma, although there are various theories about volcanic craters or subsidence in the bedrock. We now know that the lake is 19 metres deep, which is surprising considering that it is only 150 metres across.

It is said that there is a channel in the depths of the lake linking it with the crypt in Lund Cathedral. Another tale relates how two giants found a place of refuge at the bottom of the lake, where they could no longer hear the sound of the church bells. Lake Odensjö is said to be like the one eye of the god Odin.

I put the book back on the shelf and returned the leaflet to its holder. The fact that the lake was said to connect up to the crypt in Lund where I had stood only a week before sealed my resolve to journey there. I didn't need a guide-book or a leaflet to tell me whether a place was somehow special or otherwise – I would just have to go there with my own senses and experience it for myself. I left the yellow house and headed out into the forest to explore the gorge.

The Skäralid valley is a gash that cuts into the planet's crust at Söderåsen. Inaccessible to machinery and useless for agriculture, this thin seam has endured unmolested by humans over the ages. Its slopes are piled with shattered chunks of scree rock and far below the ridges of the surrounding cliffs runs the freshwater stream of Skäralid. The gorge itself is a scene of wind-polished boulders, the thrusting basalt columns of extinct volcanos and the clinking sound of gneiss rocks tumbling down slopes.

I packed a lunch and walked out past the swan lake and up the steep muddy path that led into the beech forest. The night rains had turned the paths to glistening slicks of mud and I had to exercise caution as I climbed. Nobody else was about and I soon warmed up as I ascended and traced a path following the edge of the cliffs above the scree slopes that tumbled down into the gulch. It wasn't long before I came to a sign pointing directly off the cliff. Hartspring, it said. It led to a narrow path between the trees which jutted out into the canyon like a diving board made of rock.

It was here, a plaque explained, that neolithic hunters would chase harts and other large fauna to their death – hence the name, which meant 'hart leap'. I sat down on the ledge, dangling my feet into the abyss. To leap from this point would be certain death. There would be perhaps three or four seconds before your body crashed down onto the rocks below, and I imagined the wild animals springing from this ledge, defiant to the last, and then the hunting party, victorious, gazing down on their kill. I felt the fear of those ancient animals, as if it remained frozen in time at this spot. I apologised to their spirits. "It's what we do", I said, by way of explanation. The killing of a large animal would have fed many families. In death there is life.

As I sat there thinking these thoughts and looking out over the chasm with its distant stream below, a thought struck me like an arrow. In hunting and capturing the megafauna of the region these people had been permitted to survive and endure. Not only had they survived but they had thrived, borne children, fanned out across land and sea. Human numbers were low back then. These people could be my ancestors.

This strange notion stayed there at the forefront of my mind for the rest of the day's walk. When I reflected upon it, it wasn't such a stretch of the imagination that my ancestors may have lived here. After all, my surname is of Viking in origin, being a slight modification of Hepton-stall, a village in Yorkshire settled by Scandinavian migrants. In old Norse it means something like 'Valley/Place of the Rosehips' (in modern Danish it would be Hybens Sted), so I know that at least one of my ancestors came from that village at the point when surnames were introduced in England after the Norman conquest.

What's more, a DNA test had revealed that, genetically, I was more akin to a southern Scandinavian than the statistical average. (This further revealed the interesting fact that many southern Scandinavians and north Germans can trace their lineages directly back to the Middle East, which would explain why so many have dark hair as opposed to the archetypal blonde hair of the genetically distinct northerners.) Was it such a stretch to think that a distant ancestor of mine (or yours) had stood upon that ledge, bow and arrow in hand after a long chase through dense forest, looking down on the broken still-warm body of a dead hart?

Leaving the Hartspring behind, I continued on my way along the trail, called the Liagårds trail, and after about an hour or so I found the path that led down into the valley. The beeches thinned out, slowly to be replaced with other species, as I threaded my way along the narrow descending path. The valley floor was illuminated by the overhead sun when I reached it. It was lunchtime, so I sat on a large decaying trunk protruding out of a swampy pool and ate Swedish cheese and a hard-boiled egg. Dragonflies like miniature remote-controlled planes zoomed around in the air above me, pitching their colourful bodies this way and that, and the rattle of their gossamer wings added to the soundscape of running water, pipping birds and the occasional croaking frog. I still had not seen anyone all morning and it felt like I had the forest to myself.

After I had eaten I walked towards the sound of the running water. The stream was wide, almost river-like, as it tumbled over stones and around the rotting carcasses of fallen trees. Rowan ash, alder and oak sprung up in thickets making a welcome respite from the beeches. I crossed over a rickety wooden bridge – the kind that would have harboured a lurking troll had this been a children's story – and followed the path that ran alongside the wide stream, pausing every now and again when something caught my interest. Trees and bushes dripped with ripe berries in the bright sunlight and birds flew up in alarm from the river banks as I approached. The stream and the path were hemmed in on both sides by steep scree slopes, with the lower rocks being upholstered in spongy deep green moss.

I spotted something on the path – a tiny frog no bigger than a penny. When I lowered my hand it hopped aboard and I transported it away from the path, placing it gently down beside the stream. Dragonflies floated up from still pools of river water beside large ferns, giving the scene a prehistoric feel. I walked along happily for about an hour and then took a wrong turn over a bridge which led me to a dead end in an open grassy space.

Faced with either retracing my route or crossing the river I chose the latter. Shoes and socks in hand I wobbled across the knee deep river. The water was cold, almost icy, but incredibly fresh as it rushed through my toes and swirled around my calves. On the far bank I sat on a large rock in the sun while my feet dried off.

I continued to follow the river, emerging from the valley in the middle of the afternoon at the swan lake near my camp site. A few strollers were milling around and the restaurant was still open so I went inside and ordered a coffee. The girl behind the counter was a vision of fey Swedish beauty. Blonde hair, blue eyes, a diffident shyness. As she handed me a plastic spoon and told me where the milk was I tried not to look into her eyes, for it is far too easy to fall in love with Swedish girls.

I took my coffee outside and sat by the lake. Silver shimmers raced across its surface and there was the occasional plop of a fish jumping free and vanishing again into the bullseye of expanding concentric circles of its own making. Everything seemed at peace with itself. It was impossible to imagine anything bad ever happening in this place of ethereal beauty, magic and light.

Chapter 17. Animals

"Humans are amphibians – half spirit and half animal. As spirits they belong to the eternal world, but as animals they inhabit time."

– C S Lewis

That evening, when I returned to the campsite, I met a young couple with backpacks on. They looked lost, asking where they could pitch their tent and whether I was the owner. When I told them that, no, I wasn't the owner, they chose to pitch their tent on some grass just outside the campsite. "In Sweden you can camp wherever you want", said the young man, who said his name was Fabian. A German student from the Schleswig Holstein region, Fabian was travelling with Tracey, from Hong Kong, and I invited them into the cabin for a cup of coffee.

They told me they were taking a week out from university in Hamburg and had come up on the train. Fabian said he was studying business and learning Chinese. China was the place of the future, he said, adding a 'don't you think?' after he had said it. Tracey agreed that this was so, but thought that Germany might have something interesting to teach China, especially in terms of business and engineering. This was how these two exchange students had met, they told me.

I made some coffee and put it on the table. Fabian, who possessed an athletic build and looked not unlike the actor River Phoenix, said they planned to hike around the national park and then go down to the coast to watch the migrating birds crossing the strait. This, he thought, would only occupy them for a couple of days. "It's pretty small", he added.

We sat and talked for a while. Tracey was chatty and liked

to chuckle; Fabian was more serious, and seemed a little unsure about things. Presently we got onto talking about the loaded topics of energy and economics. Fabian said that he didn't think the German plan of powering the country using completely renewable energy was viable so long as they carried on importing the base load electricity from France's nuclear power stations. Tracey nodded and said that China was going 'all in' on green energy and would soon not need to rely on fossil fuels at all.

What did I think?, they asked. I said that in my opinion they shouldn't give too much value to grand pronouncements, and that a reading of history, a layman's understanding of thermodynamics, and a good dollop of intuition was probably the best guide. They both nodded, agreeing with me but adding, "That's not what we are taught at university". After a while Tracey took out a can of baked beans from a plastic bag and proceeded to eat them cold with a spoon. "You're not supposed to eat them like that", said Fabian with Teutonic disdain. "They're supposed to be hot." But Tracey just shrugged and carried on eating. "You eat all sorts of food wrong in my country", she said.

After a dinner of packet noodles and eggs I went for my customary evening ramble in the forest. I walked a little way into the gorge to find a place where I could sit and reflect. Finding a bubbling freshwater spring I sat down beside it and pulled out my diary. In doing so I startled a heron which had been wading nearby in the shallow waters, and it rose into the air with an ungainly flapping of its great wings before disappearing above the canopy. I had come to look forward to these evening moments in the forest when the few visitors had left and the woodland creatures began to emerge from their hiding places. The sudden appearance of the heron made me think about animal spirit guides and I wondered whether I might have one. I would usually have dismissed such suggestions out of hand as a figment of an overactive imagination but now, like a lot of other things that had seemed so certain, I wasn't so sure. Bill Plotkin says this about animal totems or guides:

The human unconscious often represents itself in the shape of animals. Perhaps this is because, as a species, we evolved hand in claw with creatures prowling through the tall savanna grasses, or swinging from limb to jungle limb, parting the air above us, or drifting through the waters. Animals are the Others of the outer wild. Why should we be surprised that the Others of the inner wilds prefer to take similar forms?

I wondered how I could find out if I had one and, if so, what it was. I decided to close my eyes and ask for my spirit animal to show itself. With my eyes shut I waited for several minutes until I thought I could feel another presence nearby. I hoped it would be a fox. Having a fox as a spirit guide would be cool, I thought. But when I opened my eyes there was no fox nearby. I laughed a little, thinking how silly this had all become but then, out of the corner of me eye, I caught some movement. I turned my head a little and there, on a wooden railing not more than three feet away, stood a robin. The robin, with its coppery breast and spindly legs, was looking at me with its head cocked, as they do.

I called out to it in greeting and it hopped a little closer. I was astonished. The creepy feeling I had felt with the caterpillar came back in an instant. I proffered some crumbs from the bottom of my pack, throwing them down on the path. Like a little ball of feathery energy it hopped around the crumbs but didn't seem overly impressed with my offering. "Sorry, I didn't bring any mealworms", I said. It looked up at me again with its curious eyes before fluttering up to a branch above my head and chirping its call out into the darkening forest.

I got up and began to walk back along the course of the river to the lake near the campsite and, as I walked, the robin flew with me, always staying slightly ahead on the path. It flew from bush to bough, and from rock to railing,

emitting high-pitched chirps as if to say "Follow me!".
When I reached the open field beside the lake the robin
disappeared back into the forest and I felt our encounter
was over. Later, after I had returned home to Cornwall, I
looked up the significance of robins as totems, noting the
following from the website spirit-aminals.com:

*"If a Robin has flown into your life... He signifies stimula-
tion of new growth and renewal in many areas of life. He
teaches that any changes can be made with joy, laughter
and a song in your heart. Robin shows you how to ride the
winds of passion within your heart and become independent and self-reliant through this change. Robin will teach
you how to move forward with grace, tenacity, perseverance and assertion. Are you letting go of personal dramas? Ones that no longer serve your higher purpose? Are
you exercising compassion and patience in mental, spiritual and emotional areas? Robin will teach how to incor-
porate new beginnings with faith and trust in the process.
It is time to believe in yourself and use the inspiration that
is given. Listen carefully. It is time to sing your own song
for a new period in your life."*

Maybe it was true, I thought. Moving forward with grace,
tenacity, perseverance and assertion is a skill that many of
us could do with developing.

Chapter 18. Mushrooms

"Western civilisation is a loaded gun pointed at the head of this planet."

– Terence McKenna

All in all I ended up staying at the campsite for over a week. This was far longer than I had originally intended but I got into a routine of spending the usually rainy mornings drinking coffee, reading and writing in the cabin – which felt more like a home from home as time progressed – and then passing the afternoons and evenings walking in the forest. Few people ever came into the cabin, aside from an old man who did the cleaning each morning and studiously avoided all eye contact. It almost felt like my own personal abode. On a couple of evenings I heard scuffling noises from behind a locked door, and once, a child crying. I wondered where the noises were coming from but didn't think too deeply about it.

The rains were still ongoing, although clear spells with sun had begun to occur with increasing frequency and I started to think about heading into the forest and spending the last few nights of my journey there. So, one morning I packed up my tent and got ready to leave. There was a sauna in the cabin, and I fancied having a good long steam before I set out into the forest. I went to ask Björn about turning it on and he looked perturbed. "I will do it for you", he said, "but first I will have to get the people out".

"What people?", I asked, puzzled. "As you probably know", he said conspiratorially, lowering his glasses further down his nose "there is a family in there". This was news to me. I had no idea there were people inside the cabin, although that would explain the unusual noises I had been hearing in the evenings. Later that morning, when he came to turn on the sauna for me, I saw who he meant. It was an otherwise normal looking Swedish family with three kids and a Volvo. Who were these people? Perhaps they had been hit by the financial crisis and were seeking refuge in, of all places, a sauna. I felt confused by it all, and told Björn not to disturb them, adding that I had no idea people were staying in the sauna. His face grew serious and he pulled his glasses down the bridge of his nose once more so that he could fix me directly with his eyes "There are *no* people living in the sauna, okay?" I was confused by all this, thinking that perhaps I had just misunderstood him. In any case, I sat in the sauna for an hour and steamed myself thoroughly. It felt good and cleansing. When I emerged, dripping in sweat, I forced myself to stand under the cold shower, gasping in shock as the water ran over me. Before I left the cabin I put my final pair of wet socks under the grill in the kitchen to dry them out, and when they had finished steaming I stowed them in my pack and set off into the forest.

I didn't get very far before I saw Fabian and Tracey. Their plan to camp for free had been rumbled by Björn, who had chased them on his ride-on lawnmower and threatened to call the police unless they paid him some money for camping on the bit of grass they had assumed was public land. So instead they were installed at a little picnic spot near the forest entrance. They asked me where I was going and I told them I would probably head to an old open-door farmhouse in the forest, not far from Odin's Lake. They looked excited by this idea and asked if I minded them coming along. "No, not at all", I said. "It would be good to have some company in the forest." And yet, even as I said these words I felt my heart sinking.

The solitude I was yearning for was in danger of slipping away, but I consoled myself with the idea that I could always excuse myself and walk away for a few hours at a time. We all sat down at a table outside the visitors' cafe and I spread a map of the forest on the table, pointing out

141

where I was heading. They planned to hike along the gorge during the day, they said, but would try to get to the old farmhouse by the evening. And so we parted ways. I set off into the forest once more, this time with all my belongings on my back.

Progress was slow with the heavy pack, and I moved tortoise-like up the steep and muddy trail that led to the top of the plateau. I steadied myself using the staff as I ascended, leaning my weight on it to anchor myself on the slippery path. A heavy mist had settled in but any feeling of solitude was dispelled by the presence of dozens of young teenagers flitting around in the fog like wood elves. They were running excitedly between the trees engaging in what appeared to be some kind of orienteering exercise. Some teenage boys standing on the path asked me where the Hartspring was located and I told them it was up ahead. I could tell their curiosity was piqued and they asked me what I was doing and where I was from. I told them, half-jokingly, that I was on a quest to find a magic lake where I would meet the god Odin, and they seemed to accept this sagely before emitting yelps of joy and running off to chase one of their classmates.

After about half an hour I stopped to rest my back. A drink of water and a few mouthfuls of nuts restored me as I leaned against a boulder. The sound of the teenagers had receded and disappeared and I figured I was all alone again. I stood up and carried on my way once more. It really wasn't too far to the old house, probably only about a three hour walk, but it was a way I hadn't been before and the heavy pack slowed me down. The mist had cleared and I could now clearly see that I was still surrounded by beech trees.

I had by now walked in the forest many times but I had not grown tired of the way the sun lit up the canopy of the beeches in a blaze of green crowning the mottled shades of darkening brown beneath. Some of the trees had broken out in coppery autumnal glory, although for the most part they still retained their summery green leaves on this day in late August. I breathed the clean air deep into my lungs and marvelled at how amazing it was to be alive on a day such as this.

After a while I sat down by a stump near some conifers and pulled out my diary. I wrote:

As I walk, putting one foot in front of the other, my mind wanders along with the body. It's as if it is connected somehow to my feet. Beneath my soled feet are incalculable numbers of organisms, each weaving its own strand in the web of life, and thousands of miles of mycorrhizal threads knit the soil and decaying leaf matter together, conveying trillions of pulses of information in a system so complex that it makes our human-made Internet look puny and simple by comparison.

It is said that we live in the information age, and that our minds are bombarded with messages on a daily basis. But how much of this is true? Did we really evolve to be on the receiving end of a continuous and stimulatory flow of meaningless adverts, news updates and social media chatter? Does not a jaguar stalking its prey in the jungle receive and process a far greater flow of information as it moves silently through its kingdom? The information it receives is pertinent as to whether it will get a meal that day, but how much of the information we receive in our civilised setting is truly necessary for us to navigate the jungle of modern life?

Some people can forecast the weather by looking at the way the wind moves the leaves in a particular tree they know. Others can taste the end of summer on the sea breeze, or sense spring in the moisture in the air. What a lot of knowledge we have lost about how to truly live in the world, and how hard it will be to relearn it! These are the thoughts I am thinking as I put one foot in front of the other in the great beech forest.

A slight vibrating of the ground and the sudden feeling of

another presence made me look up from my diary. Along the path came a figure, sauntering along in the sun and singing to himself softly in a quiet voice. I recognised the man I had seen gathering mushrooms a few days earlier when I had fallen asleep in the grove. He was still wearing the Rage Against the Machine t-shirt and looked even more ragged than before.

As I saw him he saw me too and seemed to recognise me. I greeted him and he stopped on the track, standing over me. An impish grin was on his whiskery face and he said something to me that I didn't understand. It occurred to me that he wasn't Swedish at all and that he was probably from Eastern Europe or Russia.

"Sorry?", I said, looking up at the short stocky man with his grubby trousers and muddy boots.

He said another unrecognisable word, pointing at my diary. It seemed like he wanted to look at what I had been writing. I felt a bit unsure handing my little red diary over, like it was an invasion of privacy. But the man seemed harmless enough and so, cautiously, I handed it over. He took it and scanned the pages for a minute or two making little cooing sounds as he read. A look of great delight had settled on his face and then he giggled and read back a couple of lines I had just written in his thick slurry accent.

"Put one foot een front of ze ozza", he said.

He completed his recital in a theatrical manner, skipping over certain words and over-emphasising others. His eye movements were erratic and he seemed drunk or high, and I began to feel annoyed that I had handed him my diary. I wanted it back again from this man, the most uncouth fellow I had laid eyes on in Sweden.

"You writer?", he said.

"Maybe", I responded. "I write, you read."

This seemed to tickle him and he uttered a small giggle and handed back the diary. He then reached inside the small bag he was carrying and drew out a clear plastic bag containing something red which he handed to me.

"*Tak*", I said. The strange man giggled again like a child and put his finger to his lips. *Shhhh!* he said, like the last time I had met him. I looked at what he had given me. It was a mushroom, large and red with white spots. I knew what it was, had seen them growing in other places.

"Eat", said the man. "One zhroom one eat. Zen write."

"Do I cook it?" I asked.

"No cook", he said. "Just eat." He made a gobbling motion and then affected to go cross-eyed. It was clear what this mushroom would do to me if I ate it. "Better writing zen", he said. And with another smirk he bounded off along the path and was soon gone. I took out the mushroom and turned it over in my hand. It was like a fairytale mushroom, almost perfectly symmetrical and as glossy and red as a polished supermarket apple, with creamy white flecks standing proud of the cap. Its flesh was firm and the stem still held onto a small clod of dark soil where it had been pulled out of the ground. Placing it back in the plastic bag I stowed it in my daypack.

I reached the house in the middle of the afternoon. It was an old wooden farmhouse, abandoned years before by whoever had lived in it but still open for passers-by to sleep in. There was a main house and a series of outbuildings clustered around a grassy courtyard. In the centre of the courtyard was a hand-pumped well, its iron handle worn free of enamel from centuries of use. I put down my burden next to the well and went off to investigate the house.

The front door swung on its hinges and led straight into a sparse kitchen. Shelves lined with old newspaper pages stored a few canned goods and there was a disconnected cooker with some burned twists of matches next to it. Beside the cooker was a rusty kettle and a battered frying pan and on the countertop was a single unopened can of

Swedish Hunter lager – '*Bara en god ol*' (simply a good beer) said the label. Next to the beer on a piece of paper someone had written 'Help Yourself', with a smiley on it.

I moved into the next room, a sparsely furnished living area with a long plywood trestle table and some benches. A large open hearth stood empty save for a few charred scraps of wood, and any homeliness the room may have once possessed when the house was occupied was now long gone. The walls had been scrawled on with the same kind of graffiti with which trees are sometimes etched. The initials of lovers, dates when so-and-so was there, an anarchy sign or two, an inverted cross and an *Om* symbol. Something that looked like blood but could equally have been dried ketchup was spattered up one of the walls at head height and a pile of cigarette butts had been swept into a corner by a broom that now stood against the wall sentinel-like.

From the lounge I passed through a short hallway decorated with fading vintage patterned wallpaper and a chequered linoleum floor. The boards beneath my feet creaked as I walked and, although I didn't think there was anyone in the house I called out a tentative 'hello' just to be sure. Hearing no reply I continued to creep around, entering a spacious dormitory that was equally as sparsely furnished as the lounge. The beds were made from cheap pine and were covered with the kind of graffiti I had seen on the living room walls.

Some steps led upstairs to an upper floor that contained more beds. I looked out of the upper window down into the courtyard where my gear was leaning against the well. From up there I could see how the forest crowded in on this lonely old house in the woods. I went back down the stairs and into the kitchen.

The beer was there with its 'drink me' invitation, but I didn't feel like taking it. I had an uneasy feeling, as if I were being watched. It felt as if the house still contained the spirits of someone who had lived here and I couldn't help but wonder what had happened to them. The hairs on the back of my neck were standing up and I felt a sense of suffocation. I had a sudden urge to leave the house and get outside again.

In the courtyard I poked around looking for clues left by any previous inhabitants. Perhaps there would be a grave overgrown with ivy, or a box full of old photographs, or something. Instead I found a well-stacked wood store with axes and saws and another little sign saying 'Help Yourself' – again, with a smiley on it. There was a compost toilet too, housed in a flimsy shed and with unopened packs of toilet paper. I went back into the courtyard and tried the well. After a few rusty grinds, a trickle of water emerged and ran down a small wooden aqueduct into a pail. I collected some of the water in my hands and tasted it. It was sweet and good, so I filled my bottle with it.

The house seemed to look at me as I messed around with the well and I half expected to see a pale ghostly face at the upper window where I had stood a few minutes earlier. Perhaps I had watched too many horror movies as a teenager. Nevertheless, there was no question of staying there. This was a house that needed a large group of people to turn up and make a huge roaring fire, to fill the rooms with music and talk and laughter. It was no place for a single person to creep into like a cautious forest mouse. I wondered if Fabian and Tracey would even turn up. For some reason it seemed unlikely, but even so I wrote them a note saying that I had been there. I placed the note in the kitchen next to the can of lager and got out of the house as fast as I could. The flimsy door slammed shut behind me as I left.

Walking away from the house I felt a sense of relief. The forest felt more homely than that deserted shell with its graffiti and its feeling of ghostly presences. I would spend the night in the woods like a badger, I decided. I had, by now, finished *Soulcraft*. Much of the book had described people's experiences of undertaking vision quests in remote wilderness areas.

Vision quests are the way Native Americans have traditionally connected with nature on a deep level, usually by travelling into the arid and lonely areas of the great North American continent for days or weeks at a time with no food or shelter. The purpose of such a quest was to break down the ego through lack of food and lack of contact with the human world, to dissolve the sense of 'I' and become as one with the numinous. Practitioners often find themselves falling deeply into themselves, into the world of soul and the mysteries of nature and it is said that such experiences change people forever.

Fear, loneliness and hunger reduce a person to their essence, enabling clarity of vision and the opening up of possibilities. Often it is the young which are sent away on such vision quests in a form of initiation that will enable them to become true adults who respect the world and know their part within it. In our societies, these initiations have been replaced by graduation parties and confirmations, and other ways of welcoming the young into the adult world of debt-driven consumerism and other forms of hierarchical management.

There are those who say that by abandoning true initiatory practices our technocratic world has become disconnected from a deeper reality. That our young become adults in name only, with little understanding of or feeling for the interconnectedness of everything as a result. They end up cut off from the world and even from themselves, becoming meek and easy to control, and perhaps that's one reason why serious initiations are not a part of our culture any more. Indeed, most people would say that the idea of sending away our young on a soul quest from which some may not return would be immoral and a failure of our duty of protection.

Yet, as I write these words, today's newspaper says that 453 British soldiers, almost all of them young, have lost their lives fighting in Afghanistan, with hundreds more

148

dead in Iraq and several thousand severely injured. An epidemic of suicide and depression is sweeping the modern world. People reliant on mind-altering medications and suffering from addictions to drugs is at an all-time high, and loneliness grows like a cancer within our societies. Imagine how much more difficult it would be for politicians to wage wars, for pharmaceutical companies to claim ownership of our bodies and for media moguls to exploit our fears if a significant proportion of us had endured a heroic vision quest and were unwilling to offer ourselves up for sacrifice. Imagine how few would want to deaden their senses, to turn to alcohol and other synthetic drugs, to want to end it all.

But a vision quest was not for me. I didn't feel ready for one, and in any case I had a train to catch in only a couple of days. I wandered off the path for a while until I found a spot beneath a large tree at the top of a long slope that afforded a good vantage point of the forest below. I sat there, as still as I could, simply breathing and listening to sounds of the forest with my mind alert. It would be a long night, of that I was sure.

Chapter 19: Night shift

"But I don't want to go among mad people", Alice remarked.

"Oh, you can't help that", said the Cat: *"we're all mad here. I'm mad. You're mad"*.

"How do you know I'm mad?" said Alice.

"You must be", said the Cat, *"or you wouldn't have come here"*.

– Lewis Carroll, *Alice's Adventures in Wonderland*

I sat as still as I could. My pack was balanced against a tree and my poncho was spread beneath me to keep out the damp. As the shadows lengthened and the light bled out of the forest all was still. All, that is, except my mind, which was nurturing a growing ball of anxiety. It was irrational, of course, since there was nothing that could harm me in this forest. There were no grizzly bears, no wolves, no poisonous snakes and, as far as I was aware, there were no camouflaged hunters stalking about with rifles.

I waited for the animals to appear, hoping perhaps to spot a fox or maybe even a boar. In the silence the only sound I could hear was my own breath, punctuated every now and again by the shriek or call of a bird. A chill crept up through the forest floor and entered me, spreading like mycorrhizal tendrils. In my damp clothing I felt about ready to decompose like a pile of dead leaves and, although it was still only August, it felt more like October. I took out the thick jumper and pulled it on over my head.

By early evening it was starting to become so cold and damp that I wondered how I was going to make it through the night. And I was hungry. I didn't have much food left, save for a few biscuits and some fruit. Being cold and anxious was one thing, but adding hunger to the equation seemed a bit too much. Perhaps I should go back to the old house and see if Fabian and Tracey had turned up. But what if they weren't there, or if I got lost in the dark? I considered my options and shivered.

There was always the mushroom. I took it out of its plastic bag and turned it over in my hand. I knew it to be a fly agaric – a powerful hallucinogenic species that was commonly found in forests. I'd eaten plenty of the smaller liberty caps in my time and had never suffered from any adverse physical reaction. Would it be the same with a fly agaric? What if it caused my mind to boil up in an cauldron of psychedelic anxiety? Would I be found running naked through the woods at dawn, gibbering and drooling like a character from an H P Lovecraft story? I tried to put such thoughts aside as I broke off a chunk of flesh and raised it to my lips.

Before putting it in my mouth I paused. What does the forest say? I asked myself. I looked around me, at the trees and the dark leaves on the forest floor and I got the sensation of approval. After all, if I could stick a Max burger in my mouth and swallow it, why couldn't I do the same with something natural that people had been consuming for thousands of years? With that I popped the chunk of mushroom in my mouth and chewed. I broke the rest of it into pieces and ate them one by one, chewing a little and washing it down with the water from the well. I pondered whether I should eat the stem and ended up biting off the top half and chucking the soily base into the gathering gloom. The mushroom tasted creamy and slightly bitter. I ate a couple of biscuits afterwards to get rid of the taste.

It was about an hour before I started noticing strange things.

Velvety darkness had set in and with it my sense of foreboding had deepened. My nose and ears had gone numb, but not from the cold, and my mind was buzzing with moving images of people sitting in brightly lit living rooms enjoying doing mundane things such as watching television or talking with their children about their day at school. I tried to make them go away but, the more I tried to expel them, the brighter the images burned. Presently it seemed like all those living rooms full of smiling happy cosy people were giving off a form of intense – almost radioactive – heat that was spreading through the planet and making everything hotter. The ground underneath me felt hot to the touch and I had the impression that if I fell sideways off my poncho I would plunge down into a deep abyss.

Just what the hell was I doing, sitting here in the darkness in a damp Scandinavian forest, half paralysed with fear? I should be committed to a mental institution, a part of my mind yelled at me. I knew this part of my mind well – the cynical, negative voice that murmurs disquieting asides to my soft credulous self. I yelled back, telling it to shut up, trying to think about something else. Focusing on my breathing I brought my wayward self back under control. I prodded the ground around me to make sure it wasn't really hot or abyssal and, slowly but surely, I eased into a state of relaxation.

I thought about music. I hadn't heard a single note of music for about a week. This might not sound like a long time but it felt like it. Somewhere in my pack, I thought, was the peculiar little cube that stored much of my music in the form of tiny specks of static electricity. If the battery hadn't been dead right then I might have rummaged for it and turned on something suitably atmospheric to complement my forest night sit. Edvard Greig's *Peer Gynt*, perhaps, or Sinead O'Connor's *Theology* album – these were the two last pieces of music I had been listening to on that first night in inhospitable Kongelund, back near Copenhagen, under the flight path of the jumbo jets and with the caterpillar outside my tent building its chrysalis.

Just remembering the caterpillar brought it dancing back into my mind, larger than ever and glowing brightly. It was looking at me in the same quizzical way as in Kongelund, and it was munching on something, its little cheeks bulging as it chewed. When I looked closer I could see what it was eating: music. It's difficult to explain exactly what a caterpillar eating music looks like, but it was clear enough right then. I felt saddened and reflected on what this might mean. It seemed at that moment that the music of the world was waving goodbye to us. This was something I had been pondering earlier in the day – how we confidently place our trust in the longevity of the digital world, with each new format being less reliable than the one it replaces.

I thought of an album I had bought on vinyl as a teenager. I played The Cult's *Love* album so often it became scratched and unplayable. I replaced it with a cassette version, but that too eventually wore thin and broke. I had replaced it with a newer tape. The new one followed me round with my other possessions for years until it became just another piece of dusty junk that I jettisoned when nobody owned tape recorders any more. Years later, in a fit of nostalgia I had bought it on CD. It lived in my car, enabling me to sing *Brother Wolf and Sister Moon* at the top of my lungs as I drove to the corporate energy behemoth where I worked. But car life eventually scratched it beyond repair and the CD, replaced at least once, was eventually consigned to oblivion. Years later I downloaded it illegally and got a nasty computer virus into the bargain, until a couple of years ago I repurchased it for the final time as a legal download from one of the big digital providers, but later I lost the files and now the album, for me, merely exists somewhere in 'the cloud' and I can listen to it like a clairvoyant can hear the voices of the deceased.

Looking at the caterpillar in my mind, it had now been joined by thousands of others all pulsating and glowing and munching together. I dug in my pack and took out the dead iPhone and held it to my ear to see if I could hear the music inside it. Again, I thought this was mad behaviour, but it didn't seem to matter. The phone seemed to emit a soft humming noise like a fridge, but there was no music.

Instead I began to notice the sounds of the forest around me. Leaves whispered in symphonic harmony on branches high above and the trunks of the great trees creaked and groaned as if with deep ponderous voices. The radar pip of a bat sounded sharp and clear, and the mellifluous sound of the flowing water in the now far off gorge called to me through the cold air. It was as if I had asked for music, and I had been given music. I lay back on my poncho and tuned into nature's symphony.

Chapter 20. March of the snails

"We all start out knowing magic. We are born with whirlwinds, forest fires and comets inside us. We are born able to sing to birds and read the clouds and see our destiny in grains of sand. But then we get the magic educated right out of our souls. We get it churched out, spanked out, washed out, and combed out. We get put on the straight and narrow path and told to be responsible. Told to act our age. Told to grow up, for God's sake. And you know why we were told that? Because the people doing the telling were afraid of our wildness and youth, and because the magic we knew made them ashamed and sad of what they'd allowed to wither in themselves."

– Robert McCammon

Several hours must have passed. I was beginning to feel as if normality was starting to creep over the horizon of my mind once again. A million thoughts, feelings and visions had pulsated through me – most of them indescribable – but the intensity was fading. I was physically tired but the cold and damp and my lit-up mind made sleep impossible, save for a few seconds of slumber every now and again. I could feel the forest around me, a living entity that breathed out oxygen and other less-quantifiable things. Maybe I was dreaming, or perhaps I was still awake, but it seemed to me that a number of giant snails were crawling towards me through the forest.

There was more music, but this time it was human-made. The snails seemed to be moving rhythmically to Peer Gynt's *March of the Trolls*. Although this would ordinarily be an alarming thought for most people, I had a sense that these particular snails were old friends. You see, they had lived in a scrap of unsanctioned forest I had once known in Denmark – a place I called the Acid Factory Forest – and I had once decided to eat them, and then decided not to eat them. And for that, they seemed eternally grateful, even though they had died anyway.

Let me explain.

If you ever happen to find yourself flying into Copenhagen airport you will no doubt take a metro train to the city centre shortly after landing. After you have been on the eerily driverless train for roughly three minutes you will notice that to your left you are passing a built up area of characterless blocks of flats, car parks and hotels. That's where I used to live. In the other direction you'll notice that you are passing close to the sea, with Sweden clearly visible across the Øresund, if the weather is good. In the foreground, just before the shoreline, you'll notice huge mounds of dirt and tangled pieces of metal surrounded by earth moving equipment. Underneath it, although you could never tell, lies the Acid Factory Forest.

I lived next to a road called Syrefabriksvej, which in English means Acid Factory Road. The reason for this is that quite a long time ago it used to lead to – yes – an acid factory. Back in Denmark's industrial heyday the shoreline was covered with salt works, fish processing plants and factories. They said that you could dip a bucket in the sea and it would come up filled with herrings. But by the 1970s or so, the fish had all gone and the production of goods was shifting overseas. The factories shut down and the area became what is commonly called an urban wasteland.

Having a miniature rust belt did nothing for the island's reputation whatsoever. The island I lived on – the one I had spent the first night of this journey on – had always been the target of snobbery. In medieval times the contents of Copenhagen's chamber pots were brought here and spread on the land as fertiliser, and henceforth the island was known as Lorteøen – or 'shit island'. By most accounts, it was populated by a particularly coarse breed of pig farmers, and in 1521 King Christian II, who was a

156

great fan of everything Dutch, gave the southern section of the island to some farmers from Holland. His reasoning was that they could supply the royal table with quality fruit and veg – something he believed the native Danish farmers to be incapable of. The Dutch didn't have to pay taxes and, perhaps because of this, they were hated.

Amager (pronounced 'Ama' – the *ger* bit is silent – Danish is like that) continued to be unpopular for centuries. On the opening page of Søren Kierkegaard's manifesto of existentialism *Either/Or* he declares that he'd rather live on Amager talking to the pigs than live among the shallow philistines of contemporary Copenhagen society. I'm not sure if that was meant as a complement to the pigs or not.

Today the pig farms are gone and covered with apartment blocks, 7-11s, nail bars and pet grooming parlours. The shoreline, where the old acid factory was, has been given an extreme makeover and a large offshore island has been built. Fancy flats have mushroomed and the media talks about the area becoming the 'new Manhattan', whatever that might mean. Indeed, when I was living there it was common to see fashion shoots, skateboarding contests and gritty dramas being filmed down on the waterfront. It had become that kind of place. But one bit that nobody ever did anything to was the place where the old acid factory had been. It covered quite an area, and there were the remains of many other factories there too, although I never knew what they had produced. Urban legend had it that the land was poisoned, which may well have been true.

Poisoned or not, nature had been allowed to take its course over the last forty years and a forest of sorts had grown up there. I used to go there regularly to recharge my psychic batteries. Denmark, you see, is a remarkably manicured country with barely a blade of grass out of place. Maybe it's because the land was so flat and easy to tame that a cult of neatness was allowed to prosper.

But the Acid Factory Forest was different. Here there was a profusion of life. Through the concrete factory floors, the

157

tarmac car parks and silent service roads, an army of saplings had burst forth. They had soon buried what remained of decades of human endeavour beneath a blanket of leaves, twigs and earwigs. It was a place of tall silver birches, adolescent oak trees, apple trees (perhaps from people tossing cores out of passing car windows), elderberry bushes, hawthorns, dog roses and many more shrubs and trees. The place was alive with birds, and I saw some species there that I never saw anywhere else in Denmark. But mostly it was populated by a sizeable unkindness of ravens, who sat looking down philosophically from the posts that held up the rusty razor wire fence enclosing the area. Every time I saw these ravens, which was often because I used to go jogging there almost daily, I made an effort to say hello to them. After a time they grew used to me and, although I never managed to get a response out of any of them, I'm pretty sure that they understood some rudimentary English phrases after a while.

I loved visiting this wild urban forest and seeing all the flowers there in spring and the munificence of fruits and berries in the autumn. I didn't dare eat any of them – the warnings about poisoned soils were all too clear in my mind – but I was happy to just look. Once, after reading a book about wild food, I decided to harvest some snails. The snails there were unlike any others I had seen in Denmark – they were giants! And they were everywhere. I picked up about twenty and brought them back to the flat in a mason jar. My father-in-law, who is Italian and therefore knowledgeable about such matters, said that feeding them lettuce and parsley would remove the toxins, so that's what I did. I watched them slithering around for a week or two, and they watched me back with their slimy eyes on stalks. They looked so trusting and had no idea that I had plans to fry them alive in butter and garlic and invite a couple of friends around for wine and escargot.

But something had happened to make this impossible: I had grown to regard them almost as friends. I even had names for some of the more recognisable ones and so, inevitably, I couldn't bear to eat them.

After a period of desperate rationalisation, I rode my bike back down to the Acid Factory Forest and put the snails back where I had found them. The community of the forest had been reunited again. The snails had had an adventure, and had enjoyed some nice food to boot. They slithered away back to their old lives.

But then one day something dreadful happened. An invasive species was spotted in the nature zone – a predator so ruthless and pernicious that it could only spell doom to all of the ravens, foxes, squirrels and hares that called the place home. Yes, an ape-like creature wearing a hard plastic hat and a fluorescent yellow jacket was seen surveying the site with a sextant and talking into a mobile phone. A few days later more men came, as if lured by this initial colonist. They worked methodically, speaking into walkie talkies and smoking cigarettes as they drove long white stakes into the ground at 100m intervals, dividing the land up in preparation for its being brought back into the orbit of human control. The ravens remained perched on the fence and watched all of this with interest, occasionally squawking something to one another in their indecipherable tongue. It was a bad omen to be sure.

But then, just as quickly as they had come, the men went away again. For the entire winter and spring, nothing happened, and the denizens of the wasteland carried on living their lives in relative peace. But then, the next summer, I went away for a week and, when I came back I noticed something odd: all of a sudden my flat had a sea view. Where before there had been the green froth of leaves there was now the icy blue of the Baltic Sea. I got on my bike and went down to investigate.

When I got there it was a scene of utter destruction. A large machine was parked there. On its front end was attached some kind of giant pincer with chainsaws as mandibles. It had evidently been over the whole area because nothing now rose more than a foot from the ground. The debris was still there, and so were the ravens, who were all sat on the fence surveying the wreckage. Somewhere in all that tangle of branches and trunks were their nests, presumably with their young still in them.

I felt shocked, as if a family member or friend had been violently murdered. It got worse. The entire zone was sprayed with some kind of herbicide to ensure than no living thing would be left alive. Every plant and leaf went pale, wilted and fell to the ground. After a few days the whole area was nothing but dead plants and mangled wood.

I was deeply saddened. The Acid Factory Forest had given me succour and strength throughout the times I had felt down, and now it was gone. There was nothing I could do. I mentioned it to a few local people but they were all unsympathetic. "Oh it was just an eyesore, a wasteland", they said in so many words. It attracted crime, it was being used to dump trash, teenage joyriders burned cars in it, somebody had once been attacked there … it seemed like the place could do no good at all. There was nothing for it but to raze it to the ground and bring it back to a state of purity.

I wondered what had happened to all the resident wildlife. There was literally nowhere safe for the animals to go as the Acid Factory Forest had been surrounded variously by a sanitised beach (intersected by a busy road), Copenhagen airport, a yacht marina and sterile suburbia. Only the ravens, I imagined, could get away. And they did. After a couple of weeks spent staring at the devastation and cawing to one another they just left. En masse. I wondered how they had made the decision. When to go. Where to go. There is so much we don't understand in this world.

Over the coming weeks work went on at the site. The tree stumps were ripped up by another fearsome machine and bulldozed into great tangled piles before being loaded onto trucks and driven away. Then the ground was levelled and some kind of yellow plastic gauze was spread over the,

160

perhaps, forty acre site. After this, hundreds – thousands – of truckloads of building debris were brought in and spread on the ground. Maybe it was the remains of the tower blocks they had been enthusiastically dynamiting around the country. Then on top of the debris went about a metre of clay to cap it all off and make it appear neat. But I knew that beneath that huge mass of concrete, plastic and clay was a substrate layer of dying matter that was once a forty year-old forest.

And some snails that had once been on an adventure.

A sign had been put up outside the newly-erected wire fences depicting what was to be done to the land. There was an image of a computer-generated nature reserve and an explanation about how this related to the city's commitment to sustainable development. It showed immaculate grass with a few neat trees here and there. There were to be 'contemplation benches' for the computer-generated people who were strolling around with balmy contentment on their computer-generated faces. Beside it all would be a massive new space age aquarium called the Blue Planet with tanks filled with hammerhead sharks and stingrays taken from the wild. It was all going to be awesome.

The whole episode had depressed me, yet in time I came to regard the whole Acid Factory Forest fiasco in a philosophical way. Forty years is but a blink of an eye in natural time, and one day this place, and plenty more besides it, would again be rich and wild. I would be long gone by then and the rubble of the flat I have lived in would one day be snuffled over by packs of wild pigs, hunting for acorns from the oak trees I had been surreptitiously planting in municipal parks and on roadside verges around the area. More likely though, the rubble would one day soon be home to crabs, oysters, seaweed and barnacles. These were the things I had seen in my daydream vision at the Field's shopping mall on the first day of my journey.

My wistful thoughts were interrupted by something moving in the forest nearby. I turned on the small torch and a pair of green eyes glowed in the darkness. A fox. It moved away, disappearing in an instant into the blackness. I checked the time on my watch. A quarter past two. There were still some hours to go before daylight would return.

The music of the trolls was growing quieter as the effects of the mushroom lessened. The tiniest sliver of a new moon crept up above the line of the trees. I gazed at it, discerning the outline of the dark majority. Tonight, I thought, the moon was my companion. Funnily enough I didn't feel so alone in its presence. Of course, in any case, I was not alone. I was surrounded by life, by organisms that crawled in the leaf mould, that ran fleet footed through the forest, and the very trees of the forest themselves, which exhaled their cooling air and made their musical symphonies.

It occurred to me that this journey, although it had not been a long one, was characterised by my meetings with other species. I thought back to when I started out, how I had lain among the buzzing wildflowers on the site of the future stadium, the caterpillar that had startled me so, the pair of chickens in Lund, the ravens both alive and dead in my mind's eye and the robin who had waited for me to open my eyes.

Furthermore I thought about the tree that had offered me some seeds, the bushes along the way with their gorgeous berries, the peculiar cotton threadworms I had seen crossing the paths of the forest, the shiny black slugs, the eye-popping mushrooms, the swans on the lake demonstrating family love, the flapping heron waiting for a fish by the stream, the wagtails who refused my crumbs and all of the other beasts, birds and bushes that I had in some way interacted with or observed on my journey. And yes, even the bacteria in my Max burger which had so disagreed with me.

What richness of life there is, I thought, to those who simply walk outside with their eyes open. The thought reminded me of a time not too long ago when I was sitting in in a Copenhagen office block listening to some managers discussing social media strategy for the travel company I found myself working for. The words being spoken had long since become an aural blur, and I gazed around the room and realised that the only visible organic matter was what we humans were made of. Everything else, as far as I could see, was synthetic. From the computers on the plastic and metal table before us, the nylon carpet, the electric lights and overhead projector, even the very clothes we were wearing – everything was man-made.

My wandering mind played with an idea. I imagined what would happen if everything man-made simply disappeared in the blink of an eye – let's say scientists had invented the opposite of a hydrogen bomb, one that destroyed only non-organic matter. A passer-by would have noticed five naked apes hanging in mid-air with a look of startled disbelief on their faces before they came plummeting down to the ground.

The opposite would have been true where I now sat. Only the few things I had with me were human-made. All else that surrounded me was fashioned directly by the life matrix that brings form and shape to the universe (and takes it away again). And here I was, sitting in a forest in the middle of the night with all the unimaginable richness of nature living and breathing around me. What was I doing here on such a night? I felt like a naughty schoolboy who had crept from his bed in the dead of night to sit in his tree house and escape the world of school, teachers, churches and bullies.

Now that the pulsing, frenetic world of humans had gone to bed, here in the stillness of a night time forest beneath a fingernail moon, my mind soothed and stilled, it seemed as if I had slipped through a portal into another world. It was a world of webs and wonders, subtle energies and humming elegies, where matter is important but isn't even half the story.

And maybe it's as simple as that. To just hold onto the magic and not let them take it from us. I lay down and closed my eyes, breathed in the rich night air and allowed myself to be transported away into the ecstasies of a dream-fuelled sleep.

Chapter 21. The chaos-flung people

"Do not delay today's work for tomorrow."

– Arab proverb

My back was stiff and I felt somewhat bedraggled as I made my way back to the path in the cold morning light a few hours later. I knew the lake was not far away and I had a sense of trepidation for what I would find there. The woods began to thin out and then thicken again, becoming pine. The great dark green bulk of the trees enclosed me and muffled the sound of my footfalls. Nobody else was about at this hour and presently I found myself walking beside a high fence.

On the other side of it was a large open enclosure sizing several acres. Within it I could see the stumps of felled pine trees and, dotted all around, were the sprigs of young broadleaf trees. A sign on the fence read '*Forest Regeneration Project*'. I looked at the little trees poking up from within their protective plastic spirals. They were a mixture of deciduous species – a good sign that Söderåsen was growing biologically richer and that the people managing it understood the value of diversity. I felt good. All seemed to be well with the world, as if a secret orderliness had been revealed to me in the night. I rounded a bend in the path and entered an open field. To my left stood a border of mature trees which seemed to fall away down a steep slope on the far side. I knew I had arrived at the lake.

Walking closer to the trees I could see a large crater and I caught flashes of silver between the branches indicating the presence of water. Pausing, I wondered whether I should descend to the level of the lake or come back later after some breakfast. Despite the discomfort of the previous night and the fevered dreams that had accompanied my sleep, a half-baked idea had formed in my head to spend the next day and night by the lake. I would, I had decided, sit serenely by the edge of the water awaiting, perhaps, a water goddess to appear holding a sword, or something. It had seemed like a good idea the night before, but it seemed faintly idiotic now, famished as I was with hunger and so cold I could no longer feel my toes.

My dithering however was interrupted by crashing sounds in the undergrowth nearby and the din of people shouting. Male voices were yelling something in a language I didn't understand and then, with only that brief warning, there appeared a man standing in front of me on the path. He was an African, of that it was clear, and he was wearing a leather jacket and jeans and holding a can of beer. Determined to look unperturbed by his sudden appearance I continued strolling towards him. But he appeared not to notice me and, muttering, squashed the aluminium can in his hand and tossed it back down the slope he had just scrambled up. With both hands now free he proceeded to unzip his trousers and urinate copiously on a tree trunk.

By this point I was almost level with him and, not wanting to startle him the way he had done me, I called out a greeting. Only then did the man seem to notice me. He turned and looked over his shoulder at me, a pair of rheumy bloodshot eyes betraying the fact that he was absolutely, totally, completely blitzed. He croaked a sheepish 'hi' back to me and zipped himself up again, leaning on the tree for support. Voices below called out to him and he answered them before crashing back into the undergrowth. I stood for a couple of minutes, listening to the commotion down at the lake. I couldn't see any of them but it sounded like there were five or six men down there, all in a state of some merriment. I decided this was not the best time for a spot of quiet contemplation and carried on past the lake to the nearby small town of Röstånga.

The forest ended abruptly and ejected me back into civilisation. If, that is, you could call Röstånga civilisation. I plodded around the streets looking for somewhere I might be able to get some breakfast or maybe even a bed. There was a petrol station, a supermarket, a pizzeria and a few streets of houses, but otherwise not too much else. The same highway that I had pitched my tent beside on the first week – the Riksväg 13 – also passed through Röstånga, and as I stood there another truck loaded with lumber rolled through. There was also a hotel that looked welcoming yet expensive, but my need for warmth and food was at the forefront of my concerns so I went inside in the hope of finding a cup of coffee and a pastry.

The girl on duty, presiding over an empty breakfast buffet, was accommodating if a little frosty, although in all probability I did look as if I had been dragged through a hedge backwards. Which was half true. I poured myself a coffee and sipped the sweet black liquid, savouring its restorative effect as I gazed out of a window at the empty streets. By the time I had finished my second refill and also eaten a Danish pastry (also called Vienna bread in Sweden) people in the outside world had begun to wake up and give some life to the town.

But something was odd. One might have expected the people walking the streets in a tiny town in rural Sweden to be, well, Swedish. But almost everyone I saw looked to be from the Middle East. Women wearing headscarves pushed prams, men sat on walls idly fingering worry beads and olive-skinned teenage girls giggled and chatted into their mobile phones. Among them was the occasional obviously Swedish person – an old silver-haired woman here, a blonde boy on a moped there – but the majority were clearly from somewhere else. They were all smart-casual dressed, as if they'd just stepped out of an H&M store. "What's going on?", I asked the girl behind the breakfast bar who, in other circumstances, could have been a catwalk model and perhaps was. "Are these people refugees?"

"Yes", she replied sparsely. "There is a centre here."

I asked where they had come from. "Mostly Syria, from

167

the war", she explained. "Some from Somalia." I thought back to the man I had seen earlier at the lake, about how his eyes had been so wasted. I didn't think Somalis liked to drink.

"There is nothing for them to do here", said the girl. "They are not allowed to work, so they just hang around. Some have bad habits."

I wondered if this was causing problems. Sweden, famously, is the most accommodating country in the world when it comes to taking in refugees. Its liberal policies dating back to the 1960s have been the envy of progressives the world over, and many of the Swedes I had met over the years were justifiably proud of them. But decisions about refugees were made in faraway Stockholm, and such an influx of people from a different country, with a different religion and culture, was bound to cause tension, I thought. The girl seemed to read my mind.

"Some people say there are too many for our town – we are only 800 people but we now have to support 400 refugees."

"Is this a problem?" I asked.

But the girl just shrugged. "No problem, really", she said. I tried to ask her more questions but she became tight-lipped, indicating that the matter was closed, so instead I asked her how much it cost to stay the night in the hotel. When she saw my reaction she told me there was another place nearby that would be more amenable to people 'on budgets'. I paid the bill and left. Sure enough, there was the place she was talking about. It was a splendidly grand wooden building set behind a lawn on the edge of the forest.

Painted a soft shade of yellow, the '*Vandrarhem*' – or 'home for wanderers' – looked both inviting and slightly forbidding. Like a set from a *Hammer House of Horror* film, the guesthouse was turreted and a Swedish flag flew high from a mast on the front lawn. I walked up the steps onto the porch and rang the doorbell, which echoed within. There were footsteps and the door opened. "Yes?" The woman was slim and grey-haired, spinster-like even. I asked if she had a room free for the night and she chuckled a little and said I could have the whole place to myself.

"Really, one room would be fine."

"Just one night?" she asked.

"Yes, maybe two."

"You cannot stay two nights", she replied, a little sharply. "I am fully booked tomorrow."

"Well, in that case just one night will do", I said, and stepped inside.

My room was on the downstairs floor. It was a large affair with chandeliers and a writing desk, like a hangover from a time before the modern era. Indeed, it was the polar opposite of the motel room I had stayed at in Lund. "You *did* bring your own sheets?", inquired the woman, looking me up and down as if I was something the cat had dragged in.

"Sheets?" I said. "Was I supposed to? I have a sleeping bag."

"The forest is full of bugs and fleas. We cannot have everyone just bringing them in here and spreading them about, you know."

Sheet hire was extra, it turned out. But I could use the kitchen and sit in the stately parlour and look at the pictures on the wall. One showed the building being constructed, in 1904, with some burly workmen posing in the foreground. In the background, behind the house, the forest was a collection of mere saplings, betraying the age of this section of it. I liked the house. It had creaking floorboards and was vintage Scandinavian, from a time before the mania for blank minimalism had taken over. I took a shower in a broom-cupboard bathroom down the hall and emerged wearing fresh clothes and with combed hair.

The woman introduced herself as Lise. She looked me over, now neatened and cleaned, and I felt as if her approval level of me had risen. She told me to sit down, pouring me a cup of tea and asking if I wanted some boiled eggs. "That would be great", I replied. I asked her about the house and herself. She said she was from Stockholm and had taken over the guesthouse ten years ago, spending the summers here and then shuttering it during winter. I explained who I was and what I was doing there, and she seemed interested in my chaotic caper.

"You are not like most of the guests we get here", she said. Slowly, as we talked and drank tea, the *sangfroid* began to melt away. I asked her about the old house in the woods, half expecting she would tell me the resident family had been killed by an axeman in some kind of Amityville massacre. "No", she said, "they probably just moved somewhere more comfortable".

"What about stories? Were there any tales of ghostly happenings there? People running through the woods screaming in the middle of the night?" I told her how creepy it had felt to be there, as if someone was watching me. She laughed at my suggestion. "What are you, some kind of chicken?"

"Perhaps", I admitted, laughing.

"The house is kept open for people to stay in. You do not need any money to stay there. It is our service to people like you. But, I admit, I have not lived here for many years, and I do not know everything about that old house." She took a sip of her tea and looked out of the window at a blackbird perched on a nearby branch.

I told her I wanted to go to Odin's Lake and her eyes lit up. "Did you hear about Malena Ernman?", she asked me.

"Malena who?"

"She is a very famous singer here in Sweden", Lise explained. "She sings opera and she sings jazz as well. She had a concert on Odin's Lake a few weeks ago and it was the most..." she searched for the right word, "...the most *special* concert you have ever seen."

Lise proceeded to tell me how people had come from far and wide to see Malena Ernman perform on a floating pontoon in the centre of the lake one evening. How the audience had sat on rocks in the natural amphitheatre and how, at the end, Malena Ernman, who had just performed *Min Plats på Jorden (My Place in this World)* had kicked off her shoes, gently lowered herself into the water and swum to the shore, still singing and wearing a white ball gown that billowed behind her in the illuminated waters as the piano accompaniment played on.

"Everybody was crying from the beauty of it", said Lise. "It was pure magic."

***

After I had eaten the boiled eggs and drunk the tea I went to my room and read at the desk for a while. But after my eventful night in the forest I felt heavy and weary and I couldn't concentrate, so I lay on the bed and stared at the chandelier before sleep took me. I awoke sometime after lunch. The room and house was silent so I got up and went out for a short walk into the forest.

Stopping at the local visitor centre not far from the guest-house I saw an information placard for Odin's Lake listing the species of fish that dwelled in its waters. Pinned beside it was a picture of an angler holding up a fat pike the length of his arm. It was an advert for fishing rod hire but I was transfixed by the picture of the fish. MONSTER FISK, said the flyer, which needed no translation. As a child who used to mess around on the canal at Banbury I had been told that a pike would bite off your finger given half a chance. And the pike in the Oxford canal were tiny

171

compared to this one. There would be no swimming in the lake for me, I decided.

Röstånga in the afternoon wasn't much different from Röstånga in the morning. The lumber trucks still rolled southwards on the Riksväg 13, the occasional moped or Volvo stopped at the petrol station and the streets were still scattered with bored-looking refugees. They milled around listlessly in small groups; a bunch of pram-pushing women here, a row of men sitting on a wall there. Their presence in this rural Swedish hamlet was incongruous and they seemed like actors in a movie who had turned up on the wrong set. It was as if they were waiting for something to happen, a bus to arrive, or a concert to start.

During half a lifetime of travelling the world I had noticed that in most countries people's lives are played out in public places. From Madrid to Istanbul, Guatemala City to Mumbai, it is on the streets that social interaction takes place, news is passed on, gossip is blathered, deals are done and emotions are vented. Not so in Scandinavia. The streets here are infrastructure – cold boulevards for the conveyance of people and goods from A to B. Scandinavian life takes place in private behind closed doors, and perhaps that's why these people seemed out of place.

Passing a few women on the pavement I tried to make eye contact with them. Most blocked me out but one made the briefest of contact before looking quickly away, as if embarrassed. Another group, this time teenage girls, gave me the same response. The groups were always segregated by sex. It was a curious thing, this business of casual greeting. During my perambulations around the forest, I had often come across other walkers. In Britain, nine times out of ten, walkers crossing paths in a forest would greet each other with a cheery 'morning' or 'afternoon'. In Denmark, I had found the opposite to be true, but here in Sweden it was really a 50/50 situation. On the one hand you could take the initiative and boldly say 'hi' only to be met with that steely Scandinavian look of horror that a stranger is trying to make contact with you, but on the other hand there was an equal chance that the other party would take the initiative just when you had decided it wasn't worth making yourself look a fool. After a few days of this I had learned to settle for some brief eye contact, a quick head-nod and a short 'hi' at the ready on my lips should they greet me. It was best to hedge one's bets.

But with the refugees it was a different matter. There was a barrier there; something protective was in place. I was interested in speaking to a few of them, curious to find out their stories. But it seemed that the newcomers inhabited a different world to the Swedes – a kind of parallel universe separated by a vacuum across which communication was difficult. Eventually, after wandering around the village in circles, I decided I had better find out what time the bus would come the next morning to take me back to Lund.

At the bus stop two men were talking animatedly in Arabic. They looked to be in their mid-twenties, one heavily muscular and with a crew cut, the other thin and bearded. I guessed they were friends. As I stood there studying the timetable the muscular one asked me if I had a light. He stood there with an unlit cigarette hanging from his lips and mimed striking a flint lighter with his thumb and clasped hand. I rummaged in my bag and found one, proffering it to him. He took it and lit his cigarette and then that of his friend, handing it back to me between hands pressed together as if in prayer. I asked them where they were from. "Syria", he said.

"What do you think of it here?", I asked, meaning Sweden.

"Good life", he replied, inhaling the smoke. "Good people."

It was a stupid question. I asked him another stupid question. "Why are you here?" He immediately said something to his friend, who it was clear did not understand English, and they both laughed. "Assad", he said. He thought for a moment and added "War bring us here. When Assad gone,

I go back, rebuild my house". He turned back to his friend and they continued with their fast-paced conversation and I, having noted the time of the buses, left them to it. Lise had told me there was a pizzeria nearby and I was tempted to go in and blow the rest of my money. I had seen it down a side street and decided to indulge myself.

As I neared the pizzeria a figure emerged from inside and began to walk towards me. It was a man, and he wasn't so much walking as shambling. Sporting a blonde toothbrush moustache and a mullet hairstyle, he wore a denim jacket heavily decorated with patches as he staggered towards me yelling something in a hoarse voice. I braced myself for the inevitable encounter but, strangely enough, at that moment, a door opened in a small row of flats and a woman emerged. She was wearing a padded dressing gown and had curlers in her hair, a Chihuahua dog wedged under one arm. She scolded the intoxicated man – her husband? – and led him by the arm into the flat, slamming the door behind them. Peace returned to Röstånga.

I walked into the pizzeria, which doubled as a sorry-looking bar, and walked out again. Instead I went into the supermarket and bought some rye bread and herrings and, together with a bottle of weak lager, I sat in my room and ate alone. I spent the evening reading and went to bed early. I wanted to be up with the dawn the next, my final, day in Sweden.

I went in my room and read Marcus Aurelius for a while.

"Think constantly how many doctors have died, after knitting their brows over their own patients; how many astrologers, after predicting the deaths of others, as if death were something important; how many philosophers, after endless deliberation on death or immortality; how many heroes, after the many others they killed; how many tyrants, after using their power over men's lives with monstrous insolence, as if they themselves were immortal. Think too how many whole cities have 'died' – Helice, Pompeii, Herculaneum, innumerable others. Go over now

174

all those you have known yourself, one after the other: one man follows a friend's funeral and is then laid out himself, then another follows him – and all in a brief space of time. The conclusion of this? You should always look on human life as short and cheap. Yesterday sperm: tomorrow a mummy or ashes.

"So one should pass through this tiny fragment of time in tune with nature, and leave it gladly, as an olive might fall when ripe, blessing the earth which bore it, and grateful to the tree which gave it growth.

"Be like the rocky headland on which the waves constantly break. It stands firm, and round it the seething waters are laid to rest.

"'It is my bad luck this has happened to me.' No, you should rather say: 'It is my good luck that, although this has happened to me, I can bear it without pain, neither crushed by the present nor fearful of the future'.

As I fell asleep thoughts swam around in my head like great fat pike moving through the murky depths of the lake. I felt so lucky to be alive. Every moment filled with joy. Well, most of them.

Chapter 22. Ephemeral

"Some people die at 25 and aren't buried until they're 75."

– Benjamin Franklin

Perhaps it was because of Marcus Aurelius's meditation, but in my sleep I dreamed of my father. In my dream I was in the living room of our suburban family house in Solihull, where I had lived for most of my teenage years. My father was sitting in an armchair, reading the business section of the *Daily Telegraph* and listening to Glenn Miller's *Moonlight Serenade* on the hi-fi system. A fire roared in the grate and a heavy fug of cigar smoke hung in the air and stung my eyes.

I wanted to say something to him but I found my mouth was sealed shut and, no matter how much I tried, no words would come out. He continued to sit there, bathing in the mellifluous strains of the music and occasionally taking a long slow drag on his cigar. I watched as he angled his head back slightly and allowed the white smoke to trickle languidly out, a look of serenity on his face.

This was most unusual because in actual fact my father was dead and there was no way I could have been in a room with him with my lips sealed shut – and in my dream I knew this to be so. The last time I had seen him had been in April 2012. I was standing in a field with my youngest daughter, who was seven at the time, and we were at a small farm high up on England's South Downs. In a shed nearby, lambs were struggling into life, lying in the straw, panting from the effort of being alive, while their mothers licked them and stood guard over their tiny bodies.

From our vantage point we were able to see for many miles right down to the English Channel as it glistened in the mid-afternoon sun. There, we could just make out before the shoreline the spire of Chichester Cathedral, which stuck up like a tiny spike in the vast rolling landscape that otherwise appeared devoid of all human life.

I had been living in Denmark at the time but the reason I was in England was not to visit a farm and watch as the lambs were born. For in the rolling landscape at our feet, not far from the distant cathedral, sat my father in a room. He was surrounded by people wearing white uniforms and with kindly smiles on their faces. I had visited him some hours earlier with my sister and we had put before him a photographic book featuring classic American cars from the 1950s. His eyes had wandered over all of those Buicks and Plymouths and other huge gas-chugging automobiles fitted out with leather interiors, white wall tyres and chrome trimmings – models that he himself had owned when he lived in Canada and the United States half a lifetime ago.

We watched him as he gazed at the glossy book, a nurse turning the pages for him. Enfeebled and with his mind fogged by dementia and the drugs that the doctors pumped into him in an effort to prolong his life, it was all he could do to run his finger over the pictures and mutter unintelligibly, enchanted for an instant by the memories of all those years ago. His eyes became misty as he gazed at those old cars, driven by smart-looking, carefree young men with neat hair-dos and even neater girls in the passenger seats. He had once been one of those young men and my mother, herself long since departed, had ridden beside him.

He looked at the book for some minutes, holding it in his trembling hands, and the nurse sat nearby in case of any incident, making cheery noises about his progress and coming up with practical suggestions for how we could enliven his mind. But soon it was time to go and my father shuffled off, clutching a wheeled trolley for support. The nurse gripped his arm just in case. He said goodbye to me and kissed me on the face as if I was a girl. I'm not certain he knew who I was.

He died a few weeks later, alone in his room. My sister and I set about making funeral arrangements. It occurred to us that the way most funerals were conducted these days left the mourners in something like a state of shock. Not only must they endure priestly reassurance that their dearly departed has gone up to a heaven they never believed in, but the final farewell is marked by the sounds of an electric motor starting up as the coffin rolls through a polyester curtain into a gas-fired oven to the sound of a scratched CD of Bach's classical organ works.

That wasn't what we wanted for our father, who had been a staunch atheist and who despised churches, priests and praying. So instead we arranged for a humanist ceremony. It was to take place in a small flint chapel and be conducted by an ecumenical Hospitaller descended from an order of the chivalric knights of St John. We didn't specifically request that, but he came highly recommended and, frankly, I was surprised they still existed.

A week later, on the plane flying over from Copenhagen to Gatwick, we passed over the Netherlands. Holland was instantly recognisable from the air because of the neat geometrical patterns of the fields which, from the air, give the country the appearance of a printed circuit board. The towns and cities too were visible and I was reminded of W G Sebald writing in *The Rings of Saturn* that, from a plane leaving Amsterdam's Schiphol airport, one could observe human civilisation for what it was. From that height and with all the people and cars rendered too small for the human eye to discern, one can see only our infrastructure and observe our spread over the landscape dispassionately. When seeing such a thing one instantly realises, Sebald said, that nobody could ever be in charge of such a sprawling colony of organisms. Our notions of control are revealed as a conceit.

England, when we landed there, was washed out. Flooded. Three months of near continuous rain had made rivers burst their banks and many of the fields were under water.

Nobody had ever experienced so much rain before and all the shops were sold out of wellington boots and umbrellas. Festivals and garden parties across the land had been cancelled and a kind of fatalistic, dispirited anguish had taken over. As our train trundled southwards, skirting the southern coast, I had gazed out of the window and reflected on how sodden and wretched things looked. So this is what climate change looks like for England. So much for all those dreams of turning it into the new south of France, which some people had been happily predicting. The climate was malfunctioning, that was clear enough to see.

For a week I stayed at my sister's old Victorian house, living in the top attic room and listening at night to the heavy rain beating down on the roof. We wrote a eulogy, screwed it up and wrote another one. And then another. Father John, for that was his name, asked us what poems our father would have liked to be read out. I had Googled 'poems for funerals' and read through dozens. Anything with any mention of God was out. As were poems of a sentimental nature unbefitting of a practical-minded man. The romantics were a definite no-no. In the end we drew a blank. We just had to face it – he was not a poetic type. In any case my father had once told me that death, when it comes, is like a TV set being switched off. "When it happens", he had said, "it is a black screen. Nothing".

The day of his funeral came. I had been unable to sleep for most of the night. For the last twenty years he and I had not really seen eye to eye and now it was too late to do anything about it. I had been unable to conform to the model he had wanted me to be. I was not living in a large house on the right side of town. I had not become a millionaire in my twenties. My car was an embarrassment. I lacked confidence and, in his opinion, all that money he had spent on private schooling had been a bad investment. I was a dud, and, whenever we got together, he reminded me of this. We didn't get together much.

The country hotel where the funeral was taking place was

only a short drive away. As we turned down the long cedar-lined drive we saw the hearse pulling in just in front of us. There he was. We followed it, the rain splattering against the windscreen as we drove along in silence.

Three of my cousins were there waiting for us in the chapel. I hadn't seen them in sixteen years. Now they were all greying, middle-aged and dressed in black. My father had been the last of the generation above us – now we were the new eldest generation. That was a sobering thought. There were only twelve of us in all, for my father had few friends in his later life. After the service, which saw us sitting six-a-side around the coffin to the strains of Debussy, we retired to the sixteenth century music room. Tea was poured into china cups and little cucumber sandwiches were served on gilded plates. It was all very English. The manager, a kilt-wearing Frenchman with multiple piercings, kept popping in and out, making the whole affair seem like a missing scene from *Four Weddings and a Funeral*.

Conversations with my relatives proceeded in the standard fashion. What car was I driving? Were the wages good in Denmark? What about property prices? A small stereo in the corner played big band hits from my father's CD collection. I could almost picture him tapping his foot to the beat and saying "Those were the days of *real* music, before it all went wrong". We nibbled our cucumber sandwiches and sipped our tea.

One of our plans had been to bury his body in woodland and plant a tree over him, but it turned out that he had expressly requested cremation in his will, so that option was out. I recalled him once saying that the best thing to do with dead bodies was to throw them on the compost heap. "We're all just worm food, Jason." But due to legal considerations that was not an option either.

The day after the funeral we took delivery of a smart-looking paper shopping bag adorned with imitation Paul Smith stripes. Inside was a plastic tub containing a greyish powder that had once been my father. It sat there on the table in the dining room and nobody really wanted to go near it. It was strange to think that here were the mortal remains of a man who had loomed so large in life, reduced to occupying a plastic container with the name of a crematorium printed on it.

Later that morning I placed the urn in the car and we drove out west to the New Forest. It was here in this vast forest, covering a hundred and fifty square miles and populated by wild ponies and pigs, that we had taken some of our caravanning holidays when I was a child. It was also here that I had first learned to ride a bicycle, and developed an early love of forests and wildness. We were pretty sure our father wouldn't mind ending up here rather than on some chemically-treated lawn in a municipal garden of remembrance.

We drove to the heart of the forest where a giant pollarded oak tree stood. It was six hundred years old and still going strong. A short path led to where it stood in a forest clearing and we were dismayed to find that a fence had been erected around it to prevent people from getting too close. We stood by the fence dithering. What were we to do? We wanted to scatter the ashes close to the tree's huge twenty-five foot diameter trunk, but the fence was designed to keep people away from this 'living monument'. As I stood there holding the pot of ashes and prevaricating, it was almost as if I heard my father's voice speaking to me. It commanded, "Stop standing there like Piffy on a rock bun and get on with it!". Without further ado we vaulted over the fence and took it in turns to disperse his ashes.

As I scattered them I felt a sense of sadness and grief; not simply because he was dead, but because we had butted heads so many times for so long. We had only done so, I now realised, because of our similarities. But the different circumstances of the external world we found ourselves living in had given us different personalities, different energies, different opinions. I felt a sense of forgiveness through the sorrow, and also a sense of gratitude. The gratitude was there because I knew that he had done his level best to turn us into individuals, unwilling to settle for the fake organ music and polyester curtains of life. He hadn't cared much about rules, or petty officials or fences. He was a man who sunbathed naked on regular beaches, who cut down his neighbour's trees because they were blocking his view, and who, on his only visit to a McDonald's, had demanded a metal knife and fork and a china plate – and got it.

A group of tourists were approaching with their cameras. We hopped back over the fence and walked back to where the car was parked. It was a hasty business, a guerrilla interring, but I knew that I would come back one quiet night when nobody else was around and when the nutrients from the ashes had leeched down into the soil and nourished the roots of that mighty oak. Perhaps I'd have a conversation with him to make up for all the conversations that we didn't have those last few years. Perhaps I'd finally get to ask him who the hell Piffy was, and why he stood on rock buns.

On the plane back to Denmark a few nights later I started to read the first edition of *The Dark Mountain Project* - which describes itself as a 'new cultural movement for an age of global disruption' - and the page fell open at an essay by one of its founders Paul Kingsnorth. The story told of his journey from child to adult and the love of the natural world his father had instilled in him. As I flew through the dark skies above the twinkling lights of the North Sea oil rigs below, I read these words, written in recollection of the long and arduous treks through the Lake District that he had taken with his father as a child:

"I look out across the moonlit Lake District ranges and it's as clear as the night air that what used to come in regular waves, pounding like the sea, comes now only in flashes, out of the corner of my eyes, like a lighthouse in a storm. Perhaps it's the way the world has changed. There are

more cars on the roads now, more satellites in the sky. The footpaths up the fells are like stone motorways, there are turbines on the moors and the farmers are being edged out by south country refugees like me, trying to escape but bringing with us the things we flee from. The new world is online and loving it, the virtual happily edging out the actual. The darkness is shut out and the night grows lighter and nobody is there to see it."

"It could be all that, but it probably isn't. It's probably me. I am 37 now. The world is smaller, more tired, more fragile, more horribly complex and full of troubles. Or, rather: the world is the same as it ever was, but I am more aware of it and of the reality of my place within it. I have grown up, and there is nothing to be done about it. The worst part of it is that I can't seem to look without thinking anymore. And now I know far more about what we are doing. We: the people. I know what we are doing, all over the world, to everything, all of the time. I know why the magic is dying. It's me. It's us."

Chapter 23. The path to Odin's Lake

"It is not death that a man should fear, but he should fear never beginning to live according to nature."

– Marcus Aurelius

I rose early, as soon as it was light enough for me to be able to see, and crept out of the old house. It had been a strange night filled with creaking floorboards and the sound of lights being turned on and off. At one point I could hear heavy breathing and it sounded like someone was in the room with me. But as far as I was aware the only two people in the house had been myself and Lise.

The path that led to the lake was nearby and I was soon on it, walking past a field of cows who stared at me with their large eyes as the grey light of dawn spread above the trees. A haze clung to the ground as I emerged into the open grassy common that bordered Odin's Lake. The tang of autumn was in the air, no doubt about it, and I hoped that I would have the lake to myself.

My heart sank as I drew near. Booming male voices once again reverberated around the common from the direction of the lake shore. As I approached them I saw it to be a group of men sat by the lake shore, middle aged and clad in brightly-coloured leisure wear. They installed around a table with cups of something steaming. I counted them, seven in all, and a very large black dog that stood at the end of their table sniffing the air. It was an immense animal, almost lion-like with its shaggy fur and huge pink tongue hanging out. I had in fact never seen such a large dog in all of my life and for a brief moment I thought it must be a bear, or perhaps a man dressed up in a pantomime costume. At the time I had no idea what breed it was but now I am able to look it up I can identify it as a caucasian mountain shepherd.

As I approached, the men and the dog turned around and regarded me. One of them called out a greeting to me. They were jovial and in high spirits, clearly out on a hiking jaunt. I returned their salutations and walked past them, skirting the shore of the lake before sitting myself down on a short pontoon jutting out over the still water. The lake was like an immaculate circular mirror, turning the surrounding trees upside down and floating the clouds beneath my dangling feet. Damsel flies hovered around the shallows and I watched them dance with mosquitos in the gathering light.

The men's voices continued to boom out in laughter, ricocheting off the caldera-like slopes that surrounded the lake before being lost in the muffling leaves of the trees. The giant monster of a dog walked over to the water and began to drink, turning itself into two giant dogs French kissing. I shut my eyes and tried to focus on clearing my mind. It seemed like I was at my journey's end and I reflected on all of the unusual events that had occurred, culminating in my sitting on the edge of this unfathomable Scandinavian lake. I thought of the people, animals and plants I had met along the way, how our paths had crossed and then diverged and that how life can look like a map of paths crossing and uncrossing again.

I heard heavy breathing behind me and opened my eyes. The giant dog stood there, looking at me with its big sad eyes. Flecks of white spit hung from its rubbery lips and, up close, I felt it could eat me with one gulp. "Come", reprimanded one of the day-hikers, noticing the dog standing over me. They had packed up their coffee cups and were walking around the rim of the lake behind me. The dog lumbered away in the direction of its master. The group leader was holding a map and eyeing the trees, looking for the path. "Sorry for disturbing you", one of them said to me in English.

"No worries, enjoy your walk", I replied.

The men and the dog blundered around for a couple of

minutes like fantasy dwarves before locating the path and disappearing into the greenery. And then it was just me. I stood up and looked around just to make sure nobody else was about. Knowing what I had to do I walked a quarter of the way around the circular lake until I came to a place where not too many reeds grew. I slipped off my shoes and socks, then my jumper, trousers and tee shirt. Giant pike or not, I knew that I had to immerse myself in this lake. The cold water shot chills up from my feet as I stepped gingerly in. Mud and stones pressed against the soles of my feet and I gasped as I strode into the deeper water and submersed my body.

As I stood chest-deep in the water I raised my arms above the surface and chanted three times. The deep low note of the druidic *Awen* reverberated off the water and the rocks, imbuing my intent with a sense of purpose and reverence. I don't know why I did this, but it felt right and, to me, this path I had chosen was the only way of being in the world that made any sense. I waded in deeper, falling forwards into a breast-stroke as the water deepened. In this way I swam around in a large circle, enjoying the feel of the water as the chill subsided and my body began to warm itself from within. But something didn't feel right. I swam back to the shore and removed my watch, my glasses and my underwear. Ha! I thought, the woman in the tourist information office had been right – maybe I was a naturist after all.

Upon re-entry my presence in the lake felt more natural. Without my glasses my sight was fuzzy and it appeared that I was moving through a pool of black and blue surrounded by green. I swam towards the centre of the lake, gliding gently through the still waters. At the centre I took in a deep breath and lay as still as I could on my back, allowing my body to be supported by the water. The fear arose within me of large fish lurking below in the depths and regarding me. I could feel them down there, sensed their cold slippery bodies and their watery eyes observing this warm fleshy morsel that had entered their domain.

There was nothing for it but to confront my fears.

I rolled over, took a deep breath and dived. Below, after the first few strokes, all was dark. I swam down, grasping at the water with my cupped hands and kicking with my legs. The pressure grew on my ears and I half expected to feel my face hitting cold mud. As I dived I exhaled, releasing a stream of bubbles that jostled and raced back to the silvery surface above. I had reached my limit. No air was left in my lungs and I hung, suspended like a newt, in the dark waters. I could see nothing around me, only the faint light from above.

There were no fish to see, no monsters or other horrors of the imagination. There was just a human being, naked as the day he was born and suspended as if *in vitrio,* out of his element and inside something else's. I thrust back towards the surface, streamlining my body for speed, and as I punctured the silver mirror that led back to my own world I gasped in lungfuls of sweet air.

I floated face-up again for some minutes until my breathing returned to normal. A slight undulating kick of the legs and a flutter of the arms was all that was needed to stop me from sinking. I closed my eyes and emptied my mind, allowing the sensation of being supported by the lake to lull me. I don't know how long I floated like this, but presently a feeling of bliss came over me. I wasn't ready for what happened next.

Something dissolved. A crack opened in infinity and the world spread out around me. It moved from the core of my body to my skin to the water and to the rocks and into the forest around the lake. From there it continued to spread, connecting with everything it came into contact with, mingling and mixing. It spread beyond our world, into the outer realms. And then something became clear to me, like a lens snapping into focus. Not so much a conscious thought but a sudden punch of feeling that needed no explanation that was simply there to be experienced and felt.

The message was presented to me, permeated me, *was* me. And the message was that we were dreaming the *wrong dream*. The dream we were dreaming was one of fear, competition, ego and separation. And the result of this is what we see around us in the world – war, environmental ruin, extinction and misery. We were creating a nightmare and if we continued on this destructive path we could expect a spiralling worsening of the outer physical world - perhaps even our own demise. It seemed like all of our destruction, all of the life we had extinguished, all the sorrow we had sown was being deeply mourned by something, perhaps the universe itself. That, on the one hand, what we were doing didn't really matter because the dream of life would continue in other invisible realms, but also that the real damage to the physical world was infinitely sad.

My eyes snapped open, perhaps in fear. I continued floating face-up on the lake, my body supported by the water, and tried to absorb what I was feeling and seeing. There I was, floating like a water lily in full flower. It seemed as if two parallel visions or dreams were floating right there with me. One was a miserable vision of darkness, of a world inhabited by foul creatures with poisoned hearts and minds where ruthlessness and evil held sway. It stank of death and decay and wasted potential; it was fearful and empty and toxic all at once. At the same time another vision seemed to hover above or around me, and this was a vision of light, powered by love, wisdom and courage. These twin perceptions of darkness and light, goodness and evil, hope and despair were entwined like two snakes locked in an endless immortal combat.

I felt infinitesimally small, an insignificant speck of conscious flesh floating in the great eye of Gaia. Everything about who I thought I was fell away in irrelevance. Nationality, age, sex, education – everything that I felt had marked me out as an individual suddenly felt superfluous, and I was left in a stripped-down state like a newborn child. Gone, too, was the illusion of control. It was a moment of connection, like summer lightning streaking silently across a hot and heavy sky. And in the same way that lightening briefly illuminates darkened landscapes, I felt that the mysterious geography of some other dimension had been momentarily revealed.

I swam back to the shore and sat there on the rocks for some time thinking about what had just happened.

How long had my experience lasted? I couldn't say – perhaps a few seconds, perhaps only a fraction of one second. Time, like many other things, had held no relevance. But, however long it lasted, in that instant it had become clear a yawning chasm had opened up. It was a black hole, a vacuum begging to be filled. And the only thing that could fill it would be people, their thoughts and their actions – people openly able to be agents of transformation who could dream an alternative reality into being and allow us to harmoniously rejoin the web of life. Shamans, we might call them. Or healers, because there's a lot of healing that needs doing.

It wouldn't matter who they were. Their task, which would require dedication, wisdom and courage, would be to create new realities using the transformative power of art, music, gardening, caring, re-wilding the margins – whatever tools were available – to fill in that void and allow us to return to balance and wholeness. We'd be welcomed with open arms as the prodigal species. This would be an urgent requisite for our continued survival, that much was clear. Yet, for now, we fixated on creating problems and then addressing the symptoms of those problems. Somehow we had to get back home. Back to a place of union and belonging. We needed catalysts to help transform our current reality into a future in which we could exist within nature's generous living arrangements.

To be an agent of transformation, a shaman able to dream a new dream, one who existed between the worlds, would not be easy. Each would have their own Gordian knot to untangle, their own battles to fight and truths to uncover.

The great Persian poet Rumi once wrote "*Forget safety. Live where you fear to live. Destroy your reputation. Be notorious*". And like Odin, the keeper of this lake, sacrifice would be required. The sacrifice of seeing the world through the easy narratives we have been fed from birth but which now threaten to destroy us. It would be a sacrifice of eyes, of sorts. But the task would not be undertaken alone, of that I felt sure.

If we failed in this respect it would not really matter to any but ourselves. Another Eastern mystic, Gandhi, said "*Whatever you do will be insignificant, but it is very important that you do it*". And it is true. By our own terms we might fail. The world will continue to progress around the sun for the next few billion years without us.

But *"whatever you do will be insignificant, but it is very important that you do it."*

If we were to destroy ourselves then equilibrium would soon return and the alterations we had made to fabric of the planet would quickly be reabsorbed into the biosphere. Yes, even the chemical, genetic and nuclear damage would one day be neutralised, and new life forms would be created out of the life matrix to fill the hole left by our passing. Intelligent beings would once more seize evolutionary niches and ascend the web of life to form mighty civilisations which then, in turn, would decay and descend into the oblivion of the great beyond. No other species would lament our passing, and yet the fact that we had once existed would remain as an eternal truth. That, I felt, was surely order of things, and it felt strangely comforting.

I looked down at my leg, noticing that the scab on my wound had fallen off, leaving nothing but purplish skin and the outline of a scar. The sound of voices awoke me from my thoughts. The day hikers were coming back. Evidently they had gone the wrong way and turned round. I quickly pulled on clothes over my wet skin and gathered my belongings. It struck me that I should leave some kind of gift. It didn't feel right to leave without some kind of offering – after all, Odin sacrificed his eye for insight.

I rummaged in my bag for something of value. The first thing my hand encountered was my iPhone. I considered for a moment tossing it into the lake – an eye for an iPhone – but I didn't want to pollute the waters. Instead I took out a Danish 20 kroner coin with the queen's head on it, and considered this instead. No, money seemed too … *human*.

I saw the staff lying there on the shore. It had accompanied me on my journey and now it was time for it to go. I lifted it up above me and threw it spear-like as far as I could. It sailed through the air and hit the surface of the lake, arrowing down beneath the surface and reappearing a few seconds later. As it floated there it bobbed gently, sending out small ripples across the surface. Damsel flies darted above it and mosquitos hovered over the shallows by the reeds at my feet. Birds flitted between branches in trees. The ripples on the surface hit the edges, rebounded a little and then died. Everything was as it should be.

As I turned to leave I bent down and picked up a stone from the edge of the lake. I slipped it into my pocket as a keepsake. It was something to reassure me that this hadn't all been some kind of dream, that something meaningful had once occurred here.

Had something happened?

Nothing had happened. Everything had happened. A random human being, a product of the techno-industrial age, raised in a culture that believes the universe to be nothing but dead matter for our own exploration and enjoyment, had swum into a small lake in a small forest in Sweden. He had glimpsed something of mystery that could not be explained by rationality and science. He had swum back and now he would leave this place and go back to his old life and things would continue pretty much as normal. He might try to forget all this nonsense about synchronic caterpillars, talking trees and magic lakes, and even if he told people about it they would laugh, slap him on the back and say "What had you been *smoking*?".

I chuckled inwardly as I walked away from the lake and back towards my everyday life, the pebble from the lake shore rubbing against my leg in my pocket. That same stone sits now on the table beside me as I type these last words in this story, which began life as a book about humans running out of oil and ended up being a curious tale about a caterpillar and a god with one eye. About how, when all is said and done, we are all woven into the fabric of the mystery of the universe together, awaiting whatever comes next and choosing whether we do so with fear or joy, or simply a sense of wonder, belonging and engagement.

Epilogue

"As wave is driven by wave
And each, pursued, pursues the wave ahead,
So time flies on and follows, flies, and follows,
Always, for ever and new. What was before
Is left behind; what never was is now;
And every passing moment is renewed."

– Ovid, *Metamorphoses*

After I had swum in the lake that day I returned to the guesthouse and had breakfast. An old man appeared from the room adjacent to mine and Lise said he had checked in late at night. This explained the creaking floorboards behind the partition wall. The man had arrived in an old Volvo, which was parked outside, and spoke no English other than a few words. Over boiled eggs and coffee he told me stories about life during the second world war. I confess I didn't understand at least half of what he was talking about, but it was clear to see that he enjoyed reminiscing. Shortly afterwards I packed up my few things and left the guesthouse.

I was waiting at the bus stop when Lise pulled up beside me and offered to give me a lift to Teckomatorp. From there I could catch the train back to Lund and Copenhagen, she said. I got in and we drove the few miles, talking about the upcoming election and what it would mean for Sweden. Dropping me off, I got my backpack from the boot of her shiny new car, realising with some embarrassment that I had left a damp patch on the passenger seat from the wet underpants I was still wearing following my swim. The rest of the journey was uneventful, and I arrived back at my mother-in-law's house later that day. The next day we flew back to Bristol airport and took the train to

Penzance, arriving late at night.

Following a good night's rest, the next morning I found myself at my desk gazing out of the window at St Michael's Mount sitting in its silver sea as foam-flecked waves broke against the granite rocks surrounding it. After a while I turned to my computer and opened a new document. I began to write, "The email from my mother-in-law came at exactly the right time."

***

Everything in the world is changing. It seems so obvious when it is put like that, but it also seems that our collective sense of security is slipping away. Maybe our sense of security was always just an illusion, a cheap conjuring trick ponied up by fossil fuels and the business of mind control as practiced by politicians, the media and the advertising industry. We have burned through half a billion years' worth of concentrated stored energy in the relative blink of an eye, and now, sitting at the peak of this extravaganza of consumption, we find ourselves staring down the long hard slope of depletion and all the challenges that brings with it. Do we tumble down the slope chaotically, howling about how unfair life is, or do we surf our way down smoothly, taking every dip and turn as we find it and in good grace?

The oil bonanza has allowed us to make societies of dizzying complexity, to put men on the moon and to expand our numbers way beyond the carrying capacity of the planet. We patted ourselves on the back and told each other stories of how great we were, that our onward march from the caves would one day take us to the stars. Scientists, without any evidence, told us the human brain was the most complex object in the universe, and some historians said that history as we knew it had ended. Economists told us that economic growth was a law of nature, like gravity, and that permanent prosperity was guaranteed if the right technicians and bankers were given full control of the machine.

But while we were busy congratulating ourselves the gremlins had begun to crawl out of the woodwork. Few people noticed that our way of life was built on predatory behaviour, the thoughtless taking of the planet's resources and the ruination of our beautiful home. It is still impolite to point out that our material wealth comes at the expense of the planetary web of life, or that people had lived in relative harmony without trashing Gaia's garden for countless millennia before the industrial revolution. Only now are we beginning to wake up and smell the gremlins.

Yet, what has been done cannot be undone. The damage we have caused is immense and the clean-up job will likely take thousands of years. We ourselves may indeed be some of the detritus that gets cleaned up. When one first realises this one is usually rightly angry. I had always had a sense that we were wrecking our home, but for most of my life I thought that common sense would prevail before it was too late. I thought that, with the right persuasion our leaders would see the light and enact policies to secure a liveable future.

I now realised that this thinking was entirely mistaken and that, as the skipper of Sea Shepherd, Paul Watson, memorably put it, we were 'an ape that has gotten out of control'. In our relentless mania for expansion, domination and control, we have brought the world to the brink of disaster, annihilated ecosystems for short term gain, polluted waterways and the seas, fugged up the skies with soot and carbon dioxide and generally acted like we had another planet we could simply move to when this one is exhausted. Which is actually what some people do believe.

The next port of call for many who have the same realisation as I had is the belief that humanity is intrinsically evil, that we were born with Original Sin and that only a benign God can save us from our folly. In the absence of such a God appearing, it is now common to hear anguished

voices decrying the human race and hoping for our immin-
ent demise. We are, in their terms, a viral menace that will
destroy all life on the planet and leave it a barren and radioactive rock spinning in the void of space. Bring on the
Apocalypse!

This seems to me to be a pretty hopeless outlook. Perhaps
it is even a doomsday cult. At its core is an anthropocentric
idea that sees us as somehow apart from nature. It indic-
ates that we are a supernatural species existing outside the
realm of what is 'natural' and therefore 'good'. I don't buy
it. Certainly we seem to be hardwired to act in the same
manner as other social primates, sharing many similarities
with baboons and other species of apes and old world
monkeys, but we also have the capacity to create great art,
to build extraordinary things and to love one another.
These are not worthless traits.

In the same manner as ants, beavers and microbes, we appeared out of the life matrix of our planet. Who's to say
that the dolphins wouldn't behave like us, given half an
evolutionary chance? And if we take that a step further and
work on the supposition that Gaia, as a whole, is a gestalt
of extraordinarily intelligent complexity, then we must by
definition have a purpose in the greater scheme. We will
almost certainly never know what that purpose is because
our minds are too small to understand it. Such thoughts are
heresy.

Perhaps, as some suggest, our specific purpose is actually
to dig up all that fossil energy, create a complex civilisation and launch space probes. Those space probes are
teeming with Earth microbes which can potentially survive
in deep space for millions of years and eventually wash up
on the surface of some distant planet at a point in the future when we ourselves are extinct and all traces of us and
our technology have melted back into the dreaming of
Gaia once again. Maybe this is our purpose, maybe not.

In any case, our planet may shake us off like a dog with a
bad case of fleas. I hope that this isn't the case – at least

not until we've had a chance to get over the 'playing with fire' stage of our evolution. But what is increasingly clear is that our way of living on this planet is unsustainable in anything but the short term and that the only real chance of our surviving in numbers large enough to enjoy a relatively complex civilisation is for us to re-learn how to live in harmony with the rest of nature. To do so will require a shift in thinking greater than that which occurred during the Enlightenment. How we get from here to there is the great challenge of our age. It's literally a case of do or die, and the only way we will get there is by abandoning our current way of thinking and taking baby steps along a path that starts right here and ends up who knows where.

None of us can do it all alone, and all silly talk of 'saving the planet' needs to be stopped now. It's we who need saving, not the world, which will get along just fine despite what we throw at it. It won't be easy along the way, and we'll almost certainly have to endure further rounds of resource wars, disease pandemics, failed ideologies and yet more dangerous technologies unleashed on the world as the current war-on-nature paradigm dies a messy death over the next century or two. Most people alive now have minds too cemented in anthropocentric orthodoxy to be able to see any other way than business as usual, and so any hope that exists lies in those who are already awake and in the generations yet to come.

It will be a long and bitter struggle, quite unlike anything we have ever come up against before, because in this case the enemy is not someone else, but ourselves. The prize at the end of the struggle will be a great shift in human consciousness, and a chance to live lightly on the Earth and enjoy the bounty that it offers. Potentially we have the chance to restore the Garden of Eden – and I don't mean that in a religious sense. But, like the best of things, such a reward will not come easily and there will be many lost along the way. Our descendants will have to live with the toxic legacy we have created for them, and it will be entirely understandable if future historians, if there are any, do actually label us as 'evil'.

With so many urgent problems bearing down on us the fight to heal the rift between humankind and nature starts right now. And the only way we can be a force for healing is if we first heal ourselves. We cannot be of much use to anyone or anything if we ourselves are burdened with depressing thoughts and feelings. As Marcus Aurelius put it:

"When you arise in the morning, think of what a precious privilege it is to be alive – to breathe, to think, to enjoy, to love".

There's something very liberating about this. It reminds me of when I was eighteen years old on my first day at university to study economics. The year was 1989 and economics was taught as a liberal arts degree, rather than the technical and market-fundamentalist way it is taught today. So, on the very first day of the course my tutor, a wild-haired Afghan man who looked somewhat like a scarecrow, told us all to go to the university bookshop and, with some of our grant money (yes, education was still free back then), buy a copy of Rousseau's *The Social Contract*, and read it before the end of the week. What, I thought slightly huffily, could an 18th century French intellectual have to teach us that would be of any value today?

I bought the book and took it back to my shabby flat in one of London's least lovely areas and began to read.

"Man is born free and everywhere he is in chains."

Show me a book with a more powerful first sentence. It struck me then as it still strikes me now because the truth of it echoes down the ages. We are born as free agents into this world, and yet everywhere we look people are shackled. The shackles are varied – debt, abusive relationships, addictions, ideologies, career pressure – but they keep so many people from truly *living*. Why is that so? It is a question that I often ask myself. What can we do to avoid falling into these traps, and how do we break the chains if we are already being held prisoner? Could a re-connection with nature be one of the answers? We have only to ask.

When I got back to Cornwall I began to research areas that had suggested themselves to me in Sweden. It seemed to me that the voice of 'nature' is desperate to speak to us and that we had better listen up. Pretty soon I found out that I wasn't the only such person doing so. People all over the world are looking to the realm of nature for answers. I gathered books and read as much as I could. Two modern day pioneers stood out to me in particular, Stephen Harrod Buhner, with his work into the intelligence of plants and healing, and Paul Stamets, with his tireless research into what fungus can teach us with regards to bioremediation – that is, healing damaged ecosystems and people. What had started out as a pretty 'out there' concept – the idea that plants and natural systems possess intelligence and that there are techniques we can learn to listen to them – is rap-idly becoming accepted as holding truth. Even formerly hard-headed scientists are now scratching their beards in puzzlement as quantum physics reveals that the simplistic billiard ball approach to understanding the universe has passed its use-by date. "Maybe Prince Charles was onto something with this crazy talking to plants stuff…", they might be heard mumbling.

This is all well and good, but we had better get a move on with regards to doing something about it. As the dimen-sions and extent of the task before us become clearer it is an understandable response of many people to simply throw up their hands in despair or jump off a bridge. A re-port by the Worldwide Fund for Nature surfaced shortly after I returned from Sweden. It stated that in just 40 years – slightly less time than I have been alive – around half of the world's wild animals, fish and birds had been wiped out by pollution, habitat loss and other human factors. The report was – briefly – big news, but was soon forgotten again in the torrent of politics, celebrity worship and other trivia that makes up the majority of what is given prominence.

Half of all wildlife wiped out in my own lifetime – and every trend accelerating towards complete annihilation. And they say it's nothing to worry about!

There are no words that are adequate to mourn such a loss. As a species we seem hell-bent on rushing towards our fate as if it didn't matter. In the mainstream media the silence is deafening when it comes to talking about the fate of the planet and the balance of life. If it is mentioned at all it is met with angry denouncements and the shooting of messengers. And yet… it is my firm belief that there is something that might be expressed as 'hope', for want of a better word. It's not the kind of hope that is peddled by those with a business plan to sell or a new miracle fuel that will allow our civilisation to continue on its trajectory. It doesn't promise that we will be able to continue our comfortable Western lifestyles forever, or that we will find some other planet to settle on (and trash – see the film *Avatar*).

Let's face it, there will be no easy way of getting back down from seven billion people, most of whom are kept alive by fossil fuels, to a population that the Earth can support. We can expect to see those four horsemen appearing with increasing regularity on all of our horizons. Into the mix we can throw climate chaos, rising sea levels, ocean acidification and a baker's dozen other catastrophes of our own making. None of that is avoidable at this stage. The only thing up for offer is how we – individually, in families or in small communities – react to it.

But if enough of us choose to take the hard route and do something about our predicament then we will find there are many salvageable dimensions to our civilisation. It requires that a critical mass of people wake up from their comfortable industrial lifestyle dream in time to do something about it. It's a kind of hope that also requires hard work: you have to *earn* it. The simple narratives of yesterday are no longer fit for purpose in the brave new world that we find ourselves living in.

We need to rapidly unlearn most of the things we have been taught about our epistemology, find new ways of living within the boundaries of our ecosystems, and jettison the whole idea that humans are a supernaturally privileged species. We'll have to find new ways of expressing ourselves, and make peace with nature once more. And all of this must be done with compassion and love, because without compassion and love nothing of lasting value can ever be achieved.

Many people have already woken up and are taking up the calling with gusto. That's why we see the likes of Gaian economics, permaculture, biodynamic agriculture, biochar production, Earth-centred spirituality and shamanic journeying experiencing a spike in interest. Hallucinogenic plant medicine can show us our place in the cosmos – although this probably isn't for everyone. We humans do not occupy centre stage in the universe, despite what René Descartes and Francis Bacon might have said. Powerful alternatives to this way of thinking are emerging and it is becoming increasingly clear to many that the rapier capitalist system which destroys both planet and people is unsustainable and will not last much longer.

One by one people are realising that any system which bestows a full half of the planet's monetary wealth to just eighty individuals is a system in serious need of an overhaul. Many are ending up dispossessed and unemployed as they realise they have been excluded from the economic system. Some can't see a way out, but many seek alternatives. Consciousness can change, but it does so slowly and only for good reason.

Whatever it is you choose to do to help heal the rift is relatively unimportant. Some will feel more drawn to certain things than others and sometimes the answer is right there underneath your feet. As I was on one of my forest walks in Sweden one day I had become aware of something around me. Like a whisper at first, I peered in the gloom at the trees, the fallen leaves and the muddy ground. When I saw it, it made me chuckle with delight. Maybe it was my subconscious mind whirring away as I walked, but it now seemed obvious to me: mushrooms. Yes, of course, they were everywhere in the forest, literally popping up around me. Mushrooms to heal, nourish and provide an income. I knew, with a resounding feeling of certainty, that I was being invited to enter the magical world of fungus. This was confirmed to me with my meetings with the strange man in the woods who gave me the fly agaric. What did he know about me that I didn't?

So it'll only be by a collective effort that we can extricate ourselves from the disastrous situation we have created. We – and by 'we' I mean you and I – must grapple with this challenge head on rather than pressing the snooze button and going back to sleep again in the hope that someone else will solve our problems. In contemplating this, I found reading Marcus Aurelius to be relevant to our task. Although he wasn't the best known, or even the most original, of the Stoic thinkers, he was a great communicator. Because stoicism, despite popular belief, is not about gritting your teeth and riding out the storm. It goes much deeper than that. It's about contemplation of nature, of our place within the greater scheme of things, and about dwelling on happiness. It does not shy away from death – and neither should we because death is but the end of one cycle and the start of another. I'm glad I put that copy of his *Meditations* in my backpack on my trip.

As we try and find our way across this new and unfamiliar landscape, we shouldn't be too hard on ourselves. There are others who will willingly do that for us. None of us is perfect and, as they say, perfection is the enemy of good. We must do what we can, each in our own unique way depending on where our interests lie, what talents we possess and what we feel drawn to. You don't have to be a sandal-wearing hippie, although you might end up one.

I am blessed in that I have a whole woodland to play in, where I can experiment with growing mushrooms, practice permaculture and bring healing energy to the landscape. Others may find themselves in completely different situations. Perhaps they have fewer resources to work with, they don't want to leave the city, they feel trapped in a dead-end job and are in debt. There is an endless variety of situations you can find yourself in at different times of your life. Nevertheless, all of us are equally capable of great creativity and imagination, and one can always plan ones escape. You don't need anyone's permission and the great thing is you will not be alone.

Something is stirring in the collective psyche as the shoddy narrative of our times becomes increasingly threadbare. The positive aspects of technology and new media are giving people access to new ideas and allowing communication on a scale never before experienced. As one by one we remove our mind-shackles and set ourselves free, we have the choice of walking away from the mess our civilisation has made of our home planet. One by one we can answer the call of our souls and extract ourselves from the cycle of destruction. One by one we can walk on our own path to our own Odin's Lakes and answer the call of our true – wild – selves. That, at least, is my hope.

We are, I believe, lucky to be alive at such a turning point in the affairs of humans and the planet which, after all, called us into being by creating us. And if you have read this far and come to the same conclusion as I have, then all I can say is good luck to you on your journey for, in truth, our paths are one and the same.

About the author

Jason Heppenstall grew up in the English Midlands and, after studying in London, got his first job working for the Chancellor of the Exchequer in H.M. Treasury's economic forecasting department. He later worked as an energy trader in the corporate world before dropping out to spend several years backpacking around the planet and teaching English. Having studied degrees in economics, computer programming and environmental policy, he settled on journalism as a second career and launched Spain's first green-focused newspaper. He was later the managing editor of the *Copenhagen Post* in Denmark and a Scandinavia correspondent for *The Guardian* newspaper. These days he lives in west Cornwall with his family and is creating a sustainable forest garden on seven acres of woodland. He enjoys mushroom cultivation, sea kayaking and writing his blog 22BillionEnergySlaves.blogspot.co.uk

Printed in Germany
by Amazon Distribution
GmbH, Leipzig